My Life in
Advertising
&
Scientific Advertising

My Life in
Advertising
&
Scientific Advertising

Two Works by Claude C. Hopkins

Mc
Graw
Hill

New York Chicago San Francisco Lisbon London Madrid Mexico City

Library of Congress Cataloging-in-Publication Data

Hopkins, Claude C., 1866–1932.
    My life in advertising ; &, Scientific advertising : two works / by Claude C. Hopkins.
        p.   cm. — (Advertising age classics library)
    Originally published: Lincolnwood, Ill., U.S.A. : NTC Business Books, 1986, © 1966.
    ISBN 0-8442-3101-0
    1. Hopkins, Claude C., 1866–1932.   2. Advertising—Biography.
  3. Advertising.   I. Hopkins, Claude C., 1866–1932. Scientific advertising.
  II. Title.   III. Title: Scientific advertising.   IV. Series.
  HF5810.H6A32   1997
  659.1'092—dc21   97-30305
                                                    CIP

36 LHN 21

ISBN 978-0-8442-3101-3
MHID   0-8442-3101-0

This book is printed on acid-free paper.

Foreword

Some one is always reprinting Claude Hopkins. In 1923 he wrote a slender book which was published by the advertising agency of Lord & Thomas (lineal antecedent of the Foote, Cone & Belding advertising agency of today). He called it "Scientific Advertising," and almost 30 years later it was re-published by Alfred Politz, eminent researcher and devotee of scientific marketing and advertising, because "the most concentrated wealth of useful discoveries [about advertising] was presented by Claude Hopkins" and because "present-day advertising research has a long way to go before it reaches the level of Claude Hopkins' contributions to efficient advertising."

In 1927 Mr. Hopkins wrote an autobiographical work, "My Life in Advertising," which first was serialized in *Advertising and Selling* magazine and subsequently was published in book form by Harper. In 1933 you could buy a copy [even one personally autographed by his widow—Claude had died in 1932] for 10 cents at almost any secondhand book store.

But by 1946 *Advertising and Selling* was reprinting the volume, with an interpretive foreword by Walter Weir, who concluded:

"There are few pages in "My Life in Advertising" which do not repay careful study—and which do not merit rereading. Before your eyes, a successful advertising life is lived—with all that went to make it successful. The lessons taught are taught exactly as they were learned. They are dished up dripping with life. It is not a book, it is an experience—and experience has always been the great teacher."

     ✻   ✻   ✻

So here we are again, reprinting Claude Hopkins, in an edition which contains both "Scientific Advertising" and "My Life in Advertising" for the edification of a generation of advertising men largely made up of the great grandchildren of Claude Hopkins and his contemporaries.

Hopkins is hopelessly out of date, and amazingly current. He was the outstanding copywriter and strategist of his time; he made $100,000 a year and more writing advertising when that kind of money was important even to the U. S. Treasury. He talked about scientific advertising in an era when there was very little science, and much of what he says seems terribly dated to the sophisticates of today. Some of it, indeed, is dated, or disproven; times and circumstances have changed. But despite it all, Claude Hopkins laid down guidelines that are too important, too eternal, to be forgotten.

The reader will find himself alternately shaking his head in violent disagreement, and applauding vigorously in complete agreement. He will be annoyed at Hopkins' conceit and arrogance, intrigued with his stories, and impressed with his short, staccato sentences—a pre-Flesch example of the best in punching home a message. Short. Simple. To the point. Like this, from the first chapter of his autobiography:

"I am sure I would fail if I tried to advertise the Rolls-Royce, Tiffany & Co. or Steinway pianos. I do not know the reactions of the rich. But I do know the common people. I love to talk to laboring-men, to study housewives who must count their pennies, to gain the confidence and learn the ambitions of poor boys and girls. Give me something which they want and I will strike the responsive chord. My words will be simple, my sentences short. Scholars may ridicule my style. The rich and vain may laugh at the factors which I feature. But in millions of humble homes the common people will read and buy. They will feel that the writer knows them. And they, in advertising, form 95 percent of our customers."

Claude Hopkins was an advertising pioneer. He blazed new trails. But he considered himself a cautious man, one who based his advertising on "fixed principles and done according to fundamentals." That is why his words are always being reprinted. That is why neophyte and expert alike will find his words stimulating, helpful, entrancing.

S. R. Bernstein, President,
Advertising Publications, Inc.

Contents

My life in advertising

Scientific advertising

My life
in advertising

CLAUDE C. HOPKINS

Preface

This book is not written as a personal history, but as a business story. I have tried to avoid trivialities and to confine myself to matters of instructive interest. The chief object behind every episode is to offer helpful suggestions to those who will follow me. And to save them some of the midnight groping which I did.

One night in Los Angeles I told this story to Ben Hampton, writer, publisher, and advertising man. He listened for hours without interruption, because he saw in this career so much of value to beginners. He never rested until he had my promise to set down the story for publication.

He was right. Any man who by a lifetime of excessive application learns more about anything than others owes a statement to successors. The

1

results of research should be recorded. Every pioneer should blaze his trail. That is all I have tried to do.

When this autobiography was announced as a serial many letters of protest came to me. Some of them came from the heads of big businesses which I had served. Behind them appeared the fear that I would claim excessive credit to the hurt of others' pride. I rewrote some of the chapters to eliminate every possible cause for such apprehensions.

No; my only claim for credit is that I have probably worked twice as long as anybody else in this field. I have lived for many years in a vortex of advertising. Naturally I learned more from experience than those who had a lesser chance. Now I want that experience, so far as possible, to help others avoid the same difficult climb. I set down these findings solely for the purpose of aiding others to start far up the heights I scaled. There is nothing to be gained for myself save that satisfaction. Had some one set down a record like this when I began I would have blessed him for it. Then, with the efforts I here describe, I might have attained some peaks in advertising beyond any of us now. May I live to see others do that.

Claude C. Hopkins.

Chapter One

Early influences

The greatest event in my career occurred a year before I was born. My father selected for me a Scotch mother. She typified in a high degree the thrift and caution, the intelligence, ambition, and energy of her race. Boys, they say, gain most of their qualities from their mothers. Certainly I inherited from mine conspicuous conservatism. The lack of that quality has wrecked more advertising men, more business men, than anything else I know.

That fact will be emphasized again and again in this book. I stress it here in tribute to the source of my prudence. "Safety first" has been my guiding star. A Scotch mother is the greatest asset a boy can have who desires a career in advertising. Then economy and caution are instinctive with him. They are fundamentals. Success, save by accident, is impossible without them. But the lack of these qualities may be partially corrected by studious cultivation.

Most business wrecks which I have encountered are due to over-reaching. To reckless speculation on a hidden chance. To that haste which laughs at conservatism. To racing ahead on unblazed trails, in fear that some rival may go farther or get higher.

There are exceptions in business, but not in advertising. All advertising disasters are due to rashness; needless and inexcusable. I do not mean advertising failures. All of us in this line attempt things which cannot be done. We are dealing with human nature, with wants, prejudices, and idiosyncrasies which we cannot measure up. No amount of experience can guide us correctly in even the majority of cases. That is why incaution is an advertising crime. In every advertising venture we are dealing with a pig in the poke.

But ordinary failures mean little. They are expected. Every advertising venture in its initial stage means simply feeling the public pulse. If people do not respond, the fault often lies with the product, or to circumstances beyond control. The loss is a trifle, if anything, in ventures which are rightly conducted. Hopes and ideas which fail to pan out are mere incidents.

I refer to catastrophes, to the crash of wild speculations. I mean advertising men who pilot some big and costly ship to the rocks. Those men rarely recover. Pilots who prove reckless are forever feared. I have seen scores of promising men in this line wreck themselves with their ships, just because they ventured with all sails spread on some uncharted course. So far as I remember, not one of them ever came back. The Scotch blood in my veins has for thirty-five years kept me from such disasters.

Because of my mother, a dime to me has always looked as big as a dollar. Not my dimes only, but the other fellow's dimes. I have spent them carefully, both as owner and trustee. I have never gambled in a large way, whether acting for myself or for others. So the failures I have made—and they are many—have never counted strongly against me. I have escaped the distrust engendered by conspicuous disaster. When I lost, I lost little in money and nothing in confidence. When I won, I often gained millions for my client and a wealth of prestige for myself. That I largely owe to my mother.

I owe her vastly more. She taught me industry. I can scarcely remember an hour, night or day, when mother was not at work. She was a college graduate with great intellectual powers. There came a time when, as a widow, she had to support her children by teaching school. Before and after school she did the housework. In the evenings she wrote books—kindergarten books for schools. When vacation came, she tramped from school to school to sell them. She did the work of three or four women. She developed three or four careers.

From my earliest years, under her direction and incentive, I did likewise. I have supported myself since the age of nine. Other boys, when they went to school as I did, counted their school work a day. It was an incident to me. Before school I opened two school-houses, built the fires and dusted the seats. After school I swept those school-houses. Then I distributed the *Detroit Evening News* to sixty-five homes before supper.

On Saturdays I scrubbed the two school-houses and distributed bills. On Sundays I was a church janitor, which kept me occupied from early morning until ten o'clock at night. In vacations I went to the farm, where the working time was sixteen hours a day.

When the doctor pronounced me too sickly for school I went to the cedar swamp. There work started at 4:30 in the morning. We milked the cows and fed the cattle before breakfast. At 6:30 we drove to the swamp, carrying our lunch with us. All day long we cut poles and hewed ties. After dinner came another milking; then we bedded the cattle for the night. At nine o'clock we crept up a ladder to the attic and our bed. Yet it never occurred to me that I was working hard.

In after years I did the same in business. I had no working hours. When I ceased before midnight, that was a holiday for me. I often left my office at two o'clock in the morning. Sundays were my best working days, because there were no interruptions. For sixteen years after entering business I rarely had an evening or a Sunday not occupied by work.

I am not advising others to follow my example. I would not advise a boy of mine to do so. Life holds so many other things more important than success that work in moderation probably brings more joy. But the man who works twice as long as his fellows is bound to go twice as far, especially in advertising.

One cannot get around that. There is some difference in brains, of course, but it is not so important as the difference in industry. The man who does two or three times the work of another learns two or three times as much. He makes more mistakes and more successes, and he learns from both. If I have gone higher than others in advertising, or done more, the fact is not due to exceptional ability, but to exceptional hours. It means that a man has sacrificed all else in life to excel in this one profession. It means a man to be pitied, rather than envied, perhaps.

Once I said in a speech, I figure that I have spent seventy years in advertising. The time is only thirty-five years by the calendar, but measured by ordinary working hours and amount of work accomplished I have lived two years in one. Frugality and caution kept me from disaster, but industry taught me advertising and made me what I am.

Through father I gained poverty, and that was another blessing. Father was the son of a clergyman. His ancestors far back had been clergymen, bred and schooled in poverty, so this was his natural state.

I owe much to that condition. It took me among the common people, of whom God made so many. I came to know them, their wants and impulses, their struggles and economies, their simplicities. Those common people whom I know so well became my future customers. When I talk to them, in print or in person, they recognize me as one of their kind.

I am sure that I could not impress the rich, for I do not know them. I have never tried to sell what they buy. I am sure I would fail if I tried to advertise the Rolls-Royce, Tiffany & Company or Steinway pianos. I do not know the reactions of the rich. But I do know the common people. I love to talk to laboring-men, to study housewives who must count their pennies, to gain the confidence and learn the ambitions of poor boys and girls. Give me something which they want and I will strike the responsive chord. My words will be simple, my sentences short. Scholars may ridicule my style. The rich and vain may laugh at the factors which I feature. But in millions of humble homes the common people will read and buy.

They will feel that the writer knows them. And they, in advertising, form 95 per cent of our customers.

To poverty I owe many experiences which taught me salesmanship. Had it not been for poverty I would never have been a house-to-house canvasser, and there I learned the most I know about human nature as applied to spending money. Canvassing is a wonderful school. One of the greatest advertising men this country has developed always went out to sell in person before he tried to sell in print. I have known him to spend weeks in going from farm to farm to learn the farmers' viewpoint. I have known him to ring a thousand door-bells to gain the woman's angle.

To poverty I owe the fact that I never went to college. I spent those four years in the school of experience instead of a school of theory. I know nothing of value which an advertising man can be taught in college. I know of many things taught there which he will need to unlearn before he can steer any practical course. Then higher education appears to me a handicap to a man whose lifetime work consists in appealing to common people.

Of course we had no advertising courses in my school days, no courses in salesmanship or journalism. I am sure it would be better if we did not have them now. I have read some of those courses. They were so misleading, so impractical, that they exasperated me. Once a man brought me from a great technical school their course in advertising, and asked me how to improve it. When I read it I said: "Burn it. You have no right to occupy a young man's most impressive years, most precious years, with rot like that. If he spends four years to learn such theories, he will spend a dozen years to unlearn them. Then he will be so far behind in the race that he will never attempt to catch up."

As I said, I was exasperated. I left a bad impression. But tell me how a college professor, who has lived his life in an educational cloister, can be fitted to teach advertising or practical business. Those things belong to the school of real business. They are learned nowhere else. I have talked with hundreds of men on this subject. I have watched the vagaries of men who, for lack of education, place a halo on men who have it. I have gone to colleges, entered their classes, listened to their lectures. I went with respect, for I belong to a college family. I was born on a college campus. Father and mother were both college graduates, my grandfather was one of the founders of a college. My sister and my daughter have college educations.

I am weighing my words. I have watched countless college men in business. In an advertising agency of which I was head, we employed college men, even as office boys. Many a client of mine has adopted the same policy—to employ none but college men. The whole idea was to employ men with training which the employers lacked, and of which they keenly felt the lack. But I cannot remember one of those men who ever gained a prominent place. The men who spent those college years in practical business had an overwhelming advantage. As far as advertising is concerned, one can learn more in one week's talk with farm folks than by a year in any classroom I know.

To Will Carleton I owe the influence which directed my course from the ministry. I was destined to be a clergyman. I came from a clerical ancestry. My given names were selected from the Who is Who of clergymen. There was not the slightest question in the minds of my family that my career would lie in the pulpit.

But they overdid the training. My grandfather was a Hardshell Baptist, my mother a Scotch Presbyterian. Together they made religion oppressive. I attended five services on Sunday. I listened Sunday evening to dreary sermons when they had to pinch me to keep me awake. Sundays were desolate days. I was not allowed to walk. I could read nothing but the Bible and the Concordance. I spent the days in counting the words and letters in the Bible to confirm the Concordance. I read in addition *Pilgrims' Progress,* and that was certainly not a guide to any road a boy would care to follow.

Seemingly every joy in life was a sin. I was taught that people who danced, played cards, or attended the theater belonged to the devil's ranks.

And they who read any books which did not come from the Sunday school were headed for a hot hereafter.

Will Carleton was a classmate of my father's at college. He wrote "Over the Hills to the Poorhouse," and other famous ballads. The state of Michigan has recently honored him by setting aside his birthday, October 23, for annual observance in the schools. He became the idol of my youth.

When I was a boy of nine or ten Will Carleton was on the lecture platform. When he came to our city he stopped at our home, and he found there the ultra-religious atmosphere not pleasant for a boy. After one of his visits he wrote a ballad based on that experience. It was published in his *City Ballads,* and the title was, "There Wasn't Any Room for His Heart." It recited the tale a young man told the sheriff on his way to prison. The tale of a Scotch Presbyterian home where religion was fanaticism. The boy, through this repression, was driven into crime. Will Carleton in that ballad made me the victim of that religious tragedy, and sent me a copy of the book.

That ballad had a greater influence on my career than all my family teachings. I admired Will Carleton. I wanted to be when I grew up a famous man like him. His attitude on my home life agreed with mine, of course. And when such a man agreed with me he gave my opinions weight. Ever after that Will Carleton became my guiding star. His attitude on religious fanaticism showed me for the first time that there was another side.

I went on studying for the ministry. I was a preacher at seventeen. I preached in Chicago at eighteen. But the course of thought which Will Carleton started eventually made a religious career impossible for me.

Another event had a great effect. My sister and I had been ill. Mother had nursed us and cared for us. During our convalescence she read to us *Uncle Tom's Cabin*. A little later I learned that the play was coming to town, so I made arrangements to distribute the bills and earn some tickets for it. After much persuasion mother agreed to let us see the play.

The time was a week ahead, and the days passed with leaden steps. On the morning of the great day I arose at four o'clock. The day seemed endless. At seven o'clock in the evening my sister and I were unable to wait longer, so we induced our mother to start with us for the town hall.

On the way we met the Presbyterian minister. He was an old bachelor who had forgotten his youth. Children instinctively shrank away from him, so I sensed in his approach a calamity.

He accosted us and said: "Well, sister, I see you are out for a stroll. I love to see a mother and her children in such perfect harmony."

Mother replied: "Yes, brother, we are out for a stroll. But for more than that. I feel I should tell you something. These children have been ill. During their recovery I read them *Uncle Tom's Cabin*. They became intensely interested. Tonight the play is coming to town and this boy has earned the tickets. I have agreed to take the children to the play. It cannot be worse than the book, and the book has certainly been a great factor for good."

The bachelor clergyman replied: "I see your logic, sister, and I sympathize with your desire. The book did prove itself a factor of tremendous good. But remember this: Those children will sometime go out from your care. They will see the lights of the devil's playhouses urging them to enter. What will they say when those temptations come? Will they say that their mother took them to their first play, so they should not hesitate?"

Mother replied: "You are right. I must not set this bad example." And she turned and took us home. In one moment I lost all respect for what mother typified, and I never regained that respect.

Another man exerted a remarkable influence on my impressive years. He was a railroad section foreman, working for $1.60 per day. He bossed several men whose wages were $1.25 per day.

Up to the age of six or seven I was surrounded by college students at play. I knew nothing of the serious side of student life, but I saw all the college pranks. Thus I gained a rather firm idea that all life was a playground.

This section foreman reversed that idea. He impressed me with the difference between him and his helpers. The helpers worked from necessity. They did as little as possible. They counted the hours to quitting time, then on Saturday nights they would go to the city and spend all they had earned in the week.

The foreman worked with enthusiasm. He said: "Boys, let us lay so many ties today. Let us get this stretch in fine shape." The men would go at it stoically, and work as though work was a bore. But the foreman made the work a game.

That man built his home in the evenings, after ten-hour days on the railroad. He cultivated a garden around it. Then he married the prettiest girl in the section, and lived a life of bliss. Eventually he was called to some higher post, but not until I learned great lessons from him.

"Look at those boys play ball," he said. "That's what I call hard work. Here I am shingling a roof. I am racing with time. I know what surface I must cover before sunset to fulfill my stint. That's my idea of fun."

"Look at those fellows whittling, discussing railroads, talking politics. The most that any of them know about a railroad is how to drive a spike. They will always do that and no more. Note what I have done while they loafed there this evening—built most of the porch on my home. Soon I will be sitting there in comfort, making love to a pretty wife. They will always be sitting on those soap boxes around the grocery stove. Which is work and which play?"

"If a thing is useful they call it work, if useless they call it play. One is as hard as the other. One can be just as much a game as the other. In both there is rivalry. There's a struggle to excel the rest. All the difference I see lies in attitude of mind."

I never forgot those talks. That man was to me what James Lucey was to Calvin Coolidge. I can say to him now, as Coolidge said, "Were it not for you I should not be here."

In later years I became a director of the Volunteers of America and made a study of life's derelicts. I studied them in the soup kitchens, in prisons and on parole. Their great trouble was not laziness, but too much love of play. Or, rather, a wrong idea of play. Most of them had in their youth worked every waking hour. But some worked at ball-throwing while others hoed the corn. Some pocketed balls while others pocketed orders. Some of their home runs were recorded in chalk while others' were carved in stone. All the difference lay in a different idea of fun.

I came to love work as other men love golf. I love it still. Many a time I beg off from a bridge game, a dinner, or a dance to spend the evening in my office. I steal away from week-end parties at my country home to enjoy a few hours at my typewriter.

So the love of work can be cultivated, just like the love of play. The terms are interchangeable. What others call work I call play, and *vice versa*. We do best what we like best. If that is chasing a polo ball, one will probably excel in that. If it means checkmating competitors, or getting a home run in something worth while, he will excel in that. So it means a great deal when a young man can come to regard his life work as the most fascinating game that he knows. And it should be. The applause of athletics dies in a moment. The applause of success gives one cheer to the grave.

Chapter Two

Lessons in advertising and selling

Father owned a newspaper in a prosperous lumbering city. The people had money to spend, so advertisers flocked there. We smile now as we remember the ads. of those days, but we smile at the hoopskirts, too.

Most of the advertisements were paid for in trade. Our home became a warehouse of advertised merchandise. I remember that at one time we had six pianos and six sewing-machines in stock.

One of the products which father advertised was Vinegar Bitters. I afterward learned its history. A vinegar-maker spoiled a batch through some queer fermentation. Thus he produced a product weird in its offensiveness. The people of those days believed that medicine must be horrible to be effective. We had oils and ointments "for man or beast" which would make either wild. We used "snake oil" and "skunk oil," presumably because of their names. Unless the cure was worse than the disease, no one would respect it.

So we had all sorts of bitters. Vinegar Bitters was the worst of its kind, and therefore the most popular. Father accepted that wretched stuff— dozens of bottles—in payment for the advertising. People came to us for pianos, organs, sewing-machines, etc., but not for medicines. So our stock of Vinegar Bitters accumulated.

Mother, being Scotch, could not tolerate waste. She was bound to use up that medicine, and I, being the sickly one of the family, was the victim. I took Vinegar Bitters morning, noon, and night. If the makers of that remedy are still in existence, I can testify that since then I have had remarkable health.

Father, in his newspaper office, also printed bills. I used to study them; sometimes I would set them. Then I would go to the advertiser and solicit the job of distributing. There were one thousand homes in our city. I would offer to place one bill in each home for $2. It meant traveling some thirty-five miles. Other boys offered to do the same job for $1.50, but they would place several bills in a home and would skip all the far-away homes. I asked advertisers to compare the results, and I soon obtained a monopoly.

That was my first experience with traced results. It taught me to stand for known and compared returns, and I have urged them ever since. In no other way can real service reveal its advantage. Doing anything blindly is folly.

When I was ten years old mother was left a widow. From that time on I had to support myself and contribute to the support of the family. I did this in many ways, but the only ways which count here are those which affected my after-career.

Mother made a silver polish. I molded it into cake form and wrapped it in pretty paper. Then I went from house to house to sell it. I found that I sold about one woman in ten by merely talking the polish at the door. But when I could get into the pantry and demonstrate the polish I sold to nearly all.

That taught me the rudiments of another lesson I never have forgotten. A good article is its own best salesman. It is uphill work to sell goods, in print or in person, without samples.

The hardest struggle of my life has been to educate advertisers to the use of samples. Or to trials of some kind. They would not think of sending out a salesman without samples. But they will spend fortunes on advertising to urge people to buy without seeing or testing. Some say that samples cost too much. Some argue that repeaters will ask for them again and again. But persuasion alone is vastly more expensive.

I wish that any advertiser who does not believe that would do what I did with that silver polish. It taught me a lesson which has saved advertisers a good many millions of dollars. It will teach any man in one day that selling without samples is many times as hard as with them.

I learned this also from street fakers. I stood for hours to listen to them in the torchlight. I realize now that I drank in their methods and theories. They never tried to sell things without demonstration. They showed in some dramatic way what the product they sold would do. It is amazing how many advertisers know less than those men about salesmanship.

I shall deal with this further. The subject is very near to my heart. I touch on it here to show where I learned the rudiments of coupons. Since then I have sent out in magazines and newspapers hundreds of millions of coupons. Some were good for a sample, some were good for a full-sized package free at any store. My name is identified with this system of advertising. I have sampled every sort of thing. Nothing else has done so much to make me a factor in advertising. Yet how simple it is and how natural. Doing what every salesman must do, every canvasser and faker. None but those who regard advertising as some magic dreamland will ever try to sell without sampling.

Another way I found to make money was by selling books. The profit was 100 per cent, and the field appeared inviting. One day I read that Allen Pinkerton, the great detective, had written his life history. No need to say that Allen Pinkerton was the hero of all boys of those times. So I induced mother to invest our little capital in a supply of Allen Pinkerton's books.

I remember when the books came in. I spread them over the floor. I was sure that all people were waiting to get them. I was anxious to rush out and supply them.

Mother said: "Get the leading men first. They will bring in the others." So I went up that morning to the mayor—Mr. Resigue—before he left his home. He received me very cordially. I was a widow's son. I had the cordial support of all our best people in my efforts to make money. And I have learned since that every young person has. A man who has made a success desires to see others make a success. A man who has worked wants to see others work. I am that way. Countless young people now flock to my home, but the welcome ones are those who work, whether young men or young women. A boy having a good time on his father's money has always been offensive to me. So, to a degree, a young woman. If there is to be any equality between the sexes, there should be equality in effort. People of either sex must justify existence. Some, through circumstances, may not fully earn their way, but they should strive to do so. I abhor drones. And I believe that my influence has driven many men and women to greater happiness.

I realize now why Mr. Resigue received me so politely that morning. I was a town boy, struggling to succeed. Never in my busiest hour have I ever refused to meet such a boy or girl myself. I have spent many precious hours with them, financed them and advised them. There is nothing I admire more than the spirit to win one's way.

But I struck a snag that morning. Mr. Resigue was a deeply religious man. He had some extreme and exacting ideals. One idea of his was that a detective, dealing with criminals, had no place in polite society. He had outgrown the hero stage.

He listened to me until I brought out my book. Then he gave it one glance, and threw the book in my lap. He said, "You are welcome in my home, but not your book. One of you must depart. You may stay here as long as you wish to, but your book must go into the street. I consider that an Allen Pinkerton book is an offense to all I stand for."

That was a revelation. I have seen it exemplified scores of times since then. Hundreds of men have discussed their pet projects with me. Boards of directors have gravely decided that the world must be on their side. I have urged them to make tests, to feel out the public pulse. I have told them that people in general could never be judged by ourselves. Some have listened and profited, some have scorned my opinions. Sometimes those who decided to judge the world by themselves, succeeded. Four times in five they failed. I know of nothing more ridiculous than gray-haired boards of directors deciding on what housewives want.

In the particular case which I recite the odds were in my favor. I went home from the mayor's house discouraged. I never dreamed that such opinions about detective stories, my loved stories, could exist.

Mother encouraged me. She said: "Go among business men; go down to the 'Big Store.' Learn what they say about it." I did so. The manager bought a book. Then he took me around among his office force and sold six more books for me. I made a big clean-up on Allen Pinkerton's book.

That taught me another lesson. We must never judge humanity by ourselves. The things we want, the things we like, may appeal to a small minority. The losses occasioned in advertising by venturing on personal preference would easily pay the national debt. We live in a democracy. On every law there are divided opinions. So in every preference, every want. Only the obstinate, the bone-headed, will venture far on personal opinion. We must submit all things in advertising, as in everything else, to the court of public opinion.

This, you will see, is the main theme of this book. I own an ocean-going yacht, but do you suppose I would venture across an ocean without a chart or compass? If I have no such records, I take soundings all the way.

We are influenced by our surroundings. The prosperous mingle with the prosperous, so do those of certain likes and inclinations. The higher we ascend the farther we proceed from ordinary humanity. That will not do in advertising.

I have seen hundreds of attempts and thousands of projects which had no chance whatever. Just because some bigoted men judged the many by the few. I have taken part in such enterprises, but only because of some business requirements. Men could not be convinced. They were going ahead on their limited conceptions, whether they were wrong or right. I have done my duty by showing them the way, or showing them the rocks, at the least possible expense.

Let me digress here to say that the road to success lies through ordinary people. They form the vast majority. The man who knows them and is one of them stands the vastly better chance.

Some of the greatest successes I have ever known in advertising were ignorant men. Two are now heads of agencies. One of them has made much money in advertising—a man who can hardly sign his name. But he knew ordinary people, and the ordinary people bought what he had to sell.

One of them wrote copy which would induce a farmer to mortgage his barn to respond. But his every sentence had to be edited for grammar.

Now college men come to us by the hundreds and say, "We have education, we have literary style." I say to them that both those things are handicaps. The great majority of men and women cannot appreciate literary style. If they do, they fear it. They fear over-influence when it comes to spending money. Any unique style excites suspicion. Any evident effort to sell creates corresponding resistance. Any appeal which seems to come from a higher class arouses their resentment. Any dictation is abhorrent to us all.

All the time we are seeking in advertising, men with the impulses of the majority. We never ask their education, never their literary qualifications. Those lacks are easily supplied. But let a man prove to us that he understands human nature and we welcome him with open arms.

Let me cite two or three examples. One day I received a letter from a man who had evidently addressed me at random. He said, "There is a great demand for ready-made meat pies, and I make them. I have named them Mrs. Brown's Meat Pies, because people like home cooking. I have created a considerable demand, and I know there exists a much larger demand. I want capital to expand it."

I saw in that man primeval instincts. His meat pies did not attract me, but his rare insight to human nature did. So I sent out a man to investigate. He found that the writer was a night cook in a shabby restaurant at $8 per week. I brought him to my office, and I offered him $25 per week to learn advertising. He came with me, and he is now one of the leading advertising men of the country.

Another man came to Chicago from Manitowoc, Wisconsin. He ate breakfast at a Thompson restaurant. He found there a baked apple which reminded him of his home. He said to himself, "There are thousands of men who come, as I do, from the country to Chicago. Two-thirds of the city consists of them. I should tell them about those baked apples."

He wrote up a page ad. on baked apples and submitted it to John R. Thompson. Mr. Thompson agreed to run it, and the patronage of his restaurants increased at once. That was the beginning of an advertising campaign which multiplied the patronage of the Thompson lunch rooms and made their owner many times a millionaire.

Most young men and most beginners think that the older men overlook them. My experience is that men in business are looking for capacity. That is the crying dearth. The more we know the more we realize the volume of work to be done. The able workers in any line are few, and all are looking for relief and help. All who see the realities are anxious to find others who can see them.

That first Thompson ad. was published on Sunday morning. I was head of the copy department in a large advertising agency. I was seeking for new talent. That very morning I found the man who wrote that ad. and brought him to my hotel. I offered him $7,500 per year—a man from a small town in Wisconsin who had never earned one-fifth that. I saw in him one of the few men who knew people as I know them.

He did not accept, for he saw in his first ad. the chance to independent success. He went on and won it. He pictured to the country boys of the city the foods they had known at home. Doughnuts, pies, real country eggs and butter. And there he laid the foundation of a great advertising career.

So with Phillip Lennan. He came from Syracuse, and after some initial experience started with Royal Tailors. The Royal Tailors sold tailored clothes to young men in small towns and in the country. Lennan conceived the idea that Chicago contained a large country population. He remembered his own environments of a few years before. Men would go to "misfit parlors" because the name suggested made-to-order clothes. So he invited the men of Chicago to come to his shops, and brought them by the tens of thousands. I offered him a position at twice what he was earning, because he knew what people really wanted.

So with Charles Mears, who advertised the Winton car. He was one of the most human men I have ever met. I offered him $25,000 per year to come into the agency field. I said: "You are one of the few natural people in advertising who appeal

to natural impulses. We need you, we who are
struggling to find real humanity."

I am trying to show by this how ordinary, how
plebeian, good advertising is. And how ordinary
humanity counts. Most new men in this field rely
on language, on the ability to express an idea.
Others count on queer things which attract attention. All of them are trying to flatter themselves,
and that always arouses resentment. The real
people in advertising whom I know are all humble
people. They came from humble people, and they
know them.

Those people are canny, economical, thrifty, sus-
picious. They are not easily fooled on ordinary
purchases. The highly-educated man, the man
who has lived in a different environment, cannot
understand them!

We see today that the heads of large enterprises
are men who arose from the ranks. They know their
associates all the way up, the men they command
and influence. Yet there is no line in which such
knowledge is more important than in advertising.
So the lowly experiences I have cited here are indicative of the chief requirements in advertising,
in business, or in politics.

Chapter Three

My start
in business

Up to my graduation from high school my ambition was the ministry. I was an earnest Bible student. The greatest game we had in our house was repeating Bible verses. We took turns, as in a spelling bee, going around the circle, until all dropped out save one. I was always that one. I had memorized more verses than anyone I met.

Often the minister dropped in, but he was no competitor of mine in a Bible competition. I knew several times as many verses. At the age of seven I was writing sermons and setting them in my father's printing-office. Often in prayer-meetings I spoke a short sermon. Thus all came to regard me as a coming pulpit orator. I was made valedictorian of my class at school. My graduating essay was on ambition, and I still remember how I denounced it, how I pleaded for poverty and service.

During the following summer I preached every Sunday in a country school where I taught. The school was twelve miles from my home, but I walked there with my luggage. I found that no one on the school board could read or write. The head of the school board and leader in his community gained his distinction through a barrel of whisky which stood in the corner of his living-room. It had floated ashore from a wreck on Lake Michigan. The man was generous with it, so his home became the headquarters of the community.

The only other furniture in the room consisted of a wood-stove and three soap boxes. Sitting on one of those soap boxes, I struggled to convince the illiterate man that I was qualified to teach. I did so at last by reading a joke from an almanac. That pamphlet constituted his entire library, and my reading of it was a revelation to him. That was another lesson. Not that I have dealt largely with illiterate people, but with very simple people. And I love them. I love and know their natural instincts and reactions.

Then came the question of pay. They were planning two months of summer school. We went to the home of the treasurer and counted the district resources. They amounted to $79.50 and I was offered that sum for my teaching.

I found a farm home which had a new organ, and two girls who wanted to play. I offered to give them music lessons, plus one dollar per week, for my board. My savings that summer amounted to $35 per month. It was a long, long time after entering business before I saved as much.

I was the teacher in that community on weekdays and the minister on Sundays. And I learned there every day new lessons about people. That, you will realize as you go along, is the most I have ever learned.

When that summer was over I went to Chicago. Mother was visiting at the home of Doctor Mills in Brighton Park, and I joined her. The day after my arrival was Sunday. In the afternoon the minister came to call. He was ill. The next day he was leaving for an extended vacation. He told us how he dreaded to preach that night, so mother suggested that I should relieve him. I was a student for the ministry.

I recognized that as a crisis. I had been growing away from mother's strict ideas of religion. I knew that she could not approve of me if she knew me as I was. She was a fundamentalist. She believed in a personal devil, in hell fire, and in all the miracles. To her the Bible was a history, inspired by its writers and to be taken literally. The earth was created in six days. Eve was derived from Adam's rib. William Jennings Bryan would have been mother's idol.

I had been growing away from her orthodox conceptions, but I had not dared to tell her. It would mean the destruction of her fondest illusions. But during the summer I had prepared a sermon based on my ideas of religion. It countenanced the harmless joys of life which had been barred to me. It argued against hell fire, against infant damnation, against the discipline I knew. It even questioned the story of the creation and of Jonah and the whale.

I resolved to deliver the sermon that night and face the consequences. I was eighteen then. Never since then have I dared to face a crisis like that. Unless I entered the ministry, I felt that my school days were ended. I had come to Chicago to decide on my course, and this was the test.

That evening in the pulpit remains one of my clearest memories. There were eight hundred people in the audience, averaging twice my age. But I forgot them all. Mother was the only auditor whom I had in mind. I knew that the minister who sat behind me was mother's friend. His orthodox ideas agreed with hers. So I felt myself a radical of the deepest dye. Never since have I faced, to my knowledge, such unanimous opposition. That sermon I consider the most daring event of my life.

As the sermon progressed the minister grew restless. Mother's face was an enigma. The audience appeared appalled. When I finished, the minister pronounced a trembling benediction. The audience filed out in silence. Not a man or woman came to greet me. Then I knew myself an outcast from the flocks I had hoped to lead.

Mother walked home in silence. She said no word to me that night, but I knew that I had brought myself to the parting of the ways. The next day she asked me to lunch with her downtown. At a table on Dearborn Street she opened the subject by stating that I no longer was her son. I waited for nothing further, but arose and walked out on the street. There I closed the door forever on a clergyman's career.

Mother was never the same to me again. She could not forgive my delinquency. We rarely met after that day. She lived to see me successful in other occupations, but she never discussed them with me. I had blighted her ambitions. But if advertising had ever been made to me as oppressive as religion, I would have abandoned that. I have, in fact, quit many a big account because of somewhat similar reasons. I believe every man should do so. No man can succeed in any line where he finds himself in disagreement and where unhappiness results. I consider business as a game and I play it as a game. That is why I have been, and still am, so devoted to it.

On that fateful day, out on Dearborn Street, I felt in my pocket and found only three dollars. The rest of my savings had been left in Michigan. I thought of Spring Lake, where my uncle had a fruit farm. It was fruit-picking time, so I resolved to get there and pick fruit.

I went down to the harbor and found several lumber vessels from Muskegon. The captain of one of them let me work my way across as choreboy in the kitchen. From Muskegon I walked to Spring Lake, and arranged to pick fruit for my uncle and others at $1.25 per day. Those earnings, with my savings as a school-teacher, gave me over $100. But I needed $200 for a course at business college.

Grandfather, who lived at my uncle's home, admired the way I worked. He called me Mr. Stick-to-itiveness. There were two of us boys on the farm, cousins of the same age. I worked sixteen hours a day, my cousin worked as little as he could. So grandfather decided to back me. All he had in the world was $100, saved to bury him. He offered that to me on condition that I assume the burial expense when it came. Of course I did.

That was another crisis in my career. There were two grandsons of similar age. So far as anyone knew, there was no choice in ability. I, being a backslider, had to face considerable disapproval. But I had saved $100, and I worked. The other boy had saved nothing, and he did not like to work. So I was the one who secured the help which changed the current of my life. The other boy became a locomotive fireman. So it has been in many a juncture I have witnessed since. The saver and the worker get the preference of the men who control opportunities. And often that preference proves to be the most important thing in life.

With $200 I went to Grand Rapids and entered Swensburg's Business College. It was a ridiculous institution. "Professor" Swensburg wrote a fine

Spencerian hand. With that single qualification he became a business teacher, but he taught us nothing. His whole conception of business as we saw it was confined to penmanship. We might as well have spent those six months in a university studying dead languages. We were supposed to graduate as bookkeepers, but all we learned of bookkeeping was some stilted figures.

The real teacher was a man named Welton. We called him "Professor" Welton. He died a janitor. His idea of teaching was to ridicule us boys and make us feel insignificant. His phrases dripped with sarcasm. His favorite form of torture was a spelling lesson with some catch words which none could spell. It showed us how hopeless we were. In one lesson, I remember, he inserted the word charavari. Not a boy could spell it. Then he asked us to consult the dictionary and bring the word in the next morning. But none of us could find it, as he knew. We could not get the first three letters right. That gave him opportunity to comment on what boobs we were.

"Professor" Swensburg gave us a morning lecture. His object seemed also to make us feel humble. Perhaps that is a good qualification for a bookkeeper who expects to grow old on a high stool. I am inclined to think it is. His lessons in humility consisted in assuring us that there were bookkeeping jobs awaiting us at $4.50 per week when our course was finished. Not a word of enlightenment, none of encouragement. Just ridicule and sarcasm directed at us students from his pompous heights. Still he rightly estimated us, I think. Anyone who paid more to a Swensburg graduate paid too much.

I was nearing the end of my course, also of my resources. I began to contemplate going back to the farm. Then one morning "Professor" Swensburg brought a postal card to his lecture, and used that as his subject. He said, "I have often told you boys that positions awaited you at $4.50 per week somewhere. Now I have the actual evidence. It comes on a postal, not in a letter, to save postage. A business man in Grand Rapids writes me that he has a bookkeeping position at $4.50 per week for one of you, and he asks me to send him a candidate. Don't all of you apply at once, but whoever among you wants that position should come to my office after the lecture and I will give him the name and address."

The other boys laughed. It was a new joke on their worthlessness. But I edged toward the door. When the "Professor" finished his lecture and started downstairs I was only one step behind.

He gave me a letter to E. G. Studley, and I went to interview him. He was interested in the Grand Rapids Felt Boot Company. The young man who had kept the books had been advanced to superintendent. They wanted some one in his place. If that superintendent considered me qualified, I could have the position.

I went to him and secured it. The bookkeeping was a minor item. I was expected to sweep the floors and wash the windows. I was also to be errand boy. The chief condition was that I was never to wear a coat. The superintendent was very democratic. He wanted no "dudes" about him. In the office and on errands downtown I was always to appear in my shirt sleeves. I could qualify for that position because I had two shirts left.

Then came the question of living on $4.50 per week. I found a small room with a widow who wanted a man in the house. That cost me one dollar per week. In a restaurant over a grocery store a dingy man served dingy meals at $2.50 per week. They were beyond my reach. I had to consider my laundry. So I arranged with him to miss two meals a week and get board for $2.25.

I was a young man, active and ever hungry. Always the great question was, what meals to miss. I tried breakfast, but morning found me starving. I tried luncheon, but that lost meal would spoil my afternoon. My only way was to race by the restaurant at night and go to bed. And that I could not do unless I crossed the street. The smell of the food would tempt me to forget the shirt sleeves which formed so great a factor in my work.

That sounds rather pitiful, but it wasn't. It was a great advance over my cedar-swamp experience. I slept alone in a bed, instead of on a hay mow with railroad section men. So long as we are going upward, nothing is a hardship. But when we start down, even from a marble mansion to a cheaper palace, that is hard.

The Felt Boot Company comprised some of the leading business men of Grand Rapids. Our sales came in winter only, so all summer long we borrowed money to get ready for those sales. The directors indorsed our notes. One of my duties was to go around and secure indorsements and renewals. In that way I met Mr. M. R. Bissell, president of the Bissell Carpet Sweeper Company.

He was a genial man, and I saw in him my chance to a higher salary. One day I waylaid him on his way to lunch. I pictured the difficulties of a young man living on $4.50 per week. There was no need to exaggerate. There on his way to lunch I told him of the two meals weekly I was obliged to miss. Above all, I pictured my dream of pie. I knew a restaurant which served pie at dinner, but the board was $3.50 per week. My greatest ambition at that time was to get that pie.

From him I learned another kink in human nature. Struggle and poverty did not appeal to him. He had known them well, and he considered them good for a fellow. But he loved pie, and had never been denied it. So he invited me home to eat pie. And he arranged for a salary of $6 per week so I could have pie every day.

Chapter Four

How I got my start in advertising

That contact with Mr. Bissell led to frequent contacts. Soon we entered the cold-weather season when my duties became heavy.

"I hear you are working hard," Mr. Bissell said to me one day.

I replied, "I should work hard, for I have so many easy months."

He insisted on the details, and he learned that I was leaving my office at two o'clock in the morning and appearing again at eight. Like all big men whom I have known, he was a tremendous worker. He had always done the average work of three men. So the hours that I kept gave him interest in me, and he urged me to join his office force.

In the early stages of our careers none can judge us by results. The shallow men judge us by likings, but they are not men to tie to. The real men judge us by our love of work, the basis of their success. They employ us for work, and our capacity for work counts above all else.

I started with the Bissell Carpet Sweeper Company in February as assistant bookkeeper at $40 a month. By November I had advanced to $75. I was head bookkeeper then, and my position offered no chance to go farther.

I began to reason in this way: A bookkeeper is an expense. In every business expenses are kept down. I could never be worth more than any other man who could do the work I did. The big salaries were paid to salesmen, to the men who brought in orders, or to the men in the factory who reduced the costs. They showed profits, and they could command a reasonable share of those profits. I saw the difference between the profit-earning and the expense side of a business, and I resolved to graduate from the debit class.

Just at that time, Mr. Charles B. Judd, our manager, brought to our accounting office a pamphlet written by John E. Powers. Powers was then the dean of advertising, which meant really a wet nurse. Advertising was then in its infancy. He had been advertising writer for John Wanamaker in Philadelphia, and there he created a new conception of advertising. He told the truth, but told it in a rugged and fascinating way. Wanamaker paid him $12,000 a year, which in those days was considered a fabulous salary. He had become the model and ideal of all men who had advertising ambitions. And so, in some respects, today. The principles for which John Powers stood are still among our advertising fundamentals.

John Powers had left Wanamaker's and gone out for himself. The Bissell Company's Eastern manager, Thomas W. Williams, was one of his great admirers. Through him I had heard a great deal of Powers and his dramatic advertising.

One incident which I remember occurred in Pittsburgh. A clothing concern was on the verge of bankruptcy. They called in Powers, and he immediately measured up the situation. He said: "There is only one way out. Tell the truth. Tell the people that you are bankrupt and that your only way to salvation lies through large and immediate sales."

The clothing dealers argued that such an announcement would bring every creditor to their doors. But Powers said: "No matter. Either tell the truth or I quit."

Their next day's ad. read something like this: "We are bankrupt. We owe $125,000, more than we can pay. This announcement will bring our creditors down on our necks. But if you come and buy tomorrow we shall have the money to meet them. If not, we go to the wall. These are the prices we are quoting to meet this situation:"

Truth was then such a rarity in advertising that this announcement created a sensation. People flocked by the thousands to buy, and the store was saved.

Another time he was asked to advertise mackintoshes which could not be disposed of.

"What is the matter with them?" Powers asked.

The buyer replied: "Between you and me they are rotten. That is nothing, of course, to say in the advertising, but it is true."

The next day came an ad. stating, "We have 1,200 rotten mackintoshes. They are almost worthless, but still worth the price we ask. Come and see them. If you find them worth the price we ask, then buy."

The buyer rushed up to Powers, ready for a fight. "What do you mean by advertising that our mackintoshes are rotten?" he cried. "How can we ever hope to sell them?"

"That is just what you told me," said Powers. "I am simply telling people the truth." Before the buyer had a chance to calm down every mackintosh was sold.

It was then, at the height of his fame, he submitted a pamphlet to the Bissell Carpet Sweeper Company, by request of Mr. Williams. It was written on butcher paper. One of Powers' ideas was that manner should never becloud matter. I well remember the first sentence—"A carpet sweeper, if you get the right one—you might as well go without matches."

But he knew nothing about carpet sweepers. He had given no study to our trade situation. He knew none of our problems. He never gave one moment to studying a woman's possible wish for a carpet sweeper.

I said to Mr. Judd, "That cannot sell carpet sweepers. There is not one word in that pamphlet which will lead women to buy. Let me try my hand. In three days I will hand you a book to compete with it, based on knowledge of our problems."

Mr. Judd smiled, but consented. During the next two nights I did not sleep at all. On the third day I presented a pamphlet which caused all to decide against Powers. He sued them for his fee, but on my pamphlet they fought and won the suit.

The carpet sweeper business was then in its infancy. Users were few and sales were small. On the strength of my pamphlet I asked for permission to try to increase the demand. Christmas was approaching. On my nights pacing the streets I had thought of the idea of a sweeper as a Christmas present. It had never been offered as such. I designed a display rack for exhibit. I drew up cards, "The Queen of Christmas Presents." And I went to the manager and asked his permission to solicit some trade by mail.

He laughed at me. He was an ex-salesman, as were all of our directors. He said: "Go out on the road and try to sell sweepers. Wherever you go you will find them covered with dust, with dealers ready to give them away. The only way to sell a new lot is to use a gun. Get a man in a corner and compel him to sign an order. When you talk of selling such men by letter, I can only laugh."

But the pamphlet I wrote had won his respect. He consented to try a few thousand letters. So I wrote and told the dealers about our display racks and our cards. I offered both free for Christmas, not as a gift, but as a reward. Not then, or ever since, have I asked a purchase. That is useless. I have simply offered service. I required a signed agreement from the dealer to display the sweepers on the rack with the cards I furnished. This made him solicit me.

I sent out some five thousand letters. They brought me one thousand orders, almost the first orders we had ever received by mail. That was the birth of a new idea which led me to graduate from the expense account to the field of money-earners.

Even then I had no courage. I did not dare to enter the business-getting field without an anchor to windward. That, again, was due to mother. So I decided to devote my days to these new adventures, and my nights to work on the books. Thus I continued for long. Rarely did I leave my office before midnight, and I often left at two in the morning.

As a boy I had studied forestry. I gathered samples of all the woods around me and sent them to other boys for exchange. Thus I accumulated scores of interesting woods. This little hobby of mine led directly to my next merchandising step.

I conceived the idea of offering Bissell Carpet Sweepers in some interesting woods. If my Christmas idea had excited ridicule, this excited pity. I asked them to build Bissell carpet sweepers in twelve distinguished woods, one in each wood to the dozen. I wanted them to run from the white of the bird's-eye maple to the dark of the walnut, and to include all the colors between.

That aroused real opposition. As I have said, all the directors of the company were ex-salesmen. One was the inventor of some new devices and was a power to be regarded. He said: "Why not talk broom action, patent dumping devices, cyco bearings, and the great things I have created?"

"I am talking to women," I replied. "They are not mechanics. I want to talk the things which they will understand and appreciate."

They finally let me do that as a concession. Since I had done what they deemed impossible and sold sweepers by letter, they could hardly refuse me a reasonable latitude. They agreed to build 250,000 sweepers, twelve woods to the dozen, for me.

While they were building the sweepers, I arranged my plans. I wrote letters to dealers, in effect as follows: "Bissell carpet sweepers are today offered twelve woods to the dozen—the twelve finest woods in the world. They come with display racks free. They come with pamphlets, like the one inclosed, to feature these twelve woods. They will never be offered again. We offer them on condition that you sign the agreement inclosed. You must display them until sold, on the racks and with the cards we furnish. You must send out our pamphlets in every package which leaves your store for three weeks." I offered a privilege, not an inducement. I appeared as a benefactor, not as a salesman. So dealers responded in a way that sold our stock of 250,000 sweepers in three weeks.

Let us pause here for a moment. That was my beginning in advertising. It was my first success. It was based on pleasing people, like everything else I have done. It sold, not only to dealers, but to users. It multiplied the use of carpet sweepers. And it gave to Bissell sweepers the practical monopoly which they maintain to this day.

Other men will still say: "I have no such opportunity. My line is not like that." Of course it isn't, but in all probability it offers a thousand advantages. No man is in any line that is harder to sell than carpet sweepers were in those days. I care not what it is. The usual advertising was impossible. A carpet sweeper would last ten years. The profit was about one dollar. Never has anyone found an ordinary way to advertise profitably an article of that class.

No young man finds himself in any field with smaller opportunity. Any man in a bank, a lumber office, a tire concern, or a grocery has a far better opportunity than I had. The only difference lies in his conceptions. I felt that clerkship was an expense, and expenses would always be minimized. I was struggling to graduate into the profit-earning class where no such limit exists.

My success with the twelve woods gave me great prestige. Then I sought other unique ideas. I went to Chicago and saw a Pullman car finished in vermilion wood. It was a beautiful red wood. I went to the Pullman factory and asked them about it. They told me that the wood came from India, that all the forests were owned by the British Government, that the wood was all cut by convicts, then hauled to the Ganges River by elephants. The vermilion wood was heavier than water, so a log of ordinary wood was placed on either side of each vermilion log to float it down the river.

That gave me the idea of an interesting picture. Government forests, convicts, elephants, the Ganges. On the way home I visualized that appeal.

But I returned to realities in Grand Rapids the next morning. My employers there had no conception of government forests, rajahs, elephants, etc. They had perfected a new dumping device.

So I argued long and loud. I asked them to order a cargo of vermilion wood. They laughed. Again they said that sweeper users were not buying woods, that they wanted broom action, efficient dumping devices, pure bristle brushes, and so forth. What folly! One might as well discuss the Einstein theory with an Eskimo.

But my successes had brought me some prestige, and I finally induced our people to order for me the single cargo I desired. While waiting for it I prepared my campaign. I had letter heads lithographed in vermilion color. My envelopes were vermilion addressed in white ink. I printed two million pamphlets with vermilion covers and a rajah's head on the front. The pamphlet told a story intended to arouse curiosity, to bring women to see that wood. No other activating factor compares with curiosity. Pictures showed the forests, the convicts, the elephants, the Ganges River and the Pullman car. One hundred thousand letters were printed to offer this wood to dealers.

After some weeks the wood arrived in the shape of rough-hewn timbers. A few hours later Mr. Johnson, the factory superintendent, came to me with tears in his eyes. "We tried to saw that vermilion wood," he said, "and the saw flew to pieces. The wood is like iron. It cannot be cut. That whole cargo is waste."

I said: "Brace up, Mr. Johnson. We all have our problems to solve. They told me I could not sell carpet sweepers by letters, but I did. Now you, as a factory expert, cannot afford to fall down."

He cut up the logs in some way with a cross-cut saw. Then he came with a new complaint. He could not drive a brad in the wood, so he saw no way to build a sweeper with it.

I said: "Johnson, you annoy me. Come, take my desk and try to sell those sweepers and I will go and make them. Bore holes for your brads."

But the storms were gathering for me. Manufacturing had almost stopped. The cost of the sweepers was mounting. So I had to make the concession of offering only three vermilion wood sweepers as part of each dozen, and the rest in ordinary woods.

Soon I was ready to mail the letters. They did not urge dealers to buy the sweepers. They offered the privilege of buying. Three vermilion wood sweepers would come in each dozen if orders were sent at once. The dealer could sell them at any price he chose. But never again could he obtain Bissell sweepers built in vermilion wood. The only condition was that the dealer must sign the agreement inclosed. He had to display the sweepers until sold, had to display the cards we sent him, and had to inclose our vermilion pamphlet in every package which left his store for three weeks. Thus again I placed the dealer in position where he was soliciting us.

The response was overwhelming. The Bissell Carpet Sweeper Company made more money in the next six weeks than they had made in any year before. They had vastly increased the number of dealers handling carpet sweepers. And they had multiplied the interest of women in a device which was then in but limited use.

After that I gave up my bookkeeping and devoted my time to selling. I sold more carpet sweepers by my one-cent letters than fourteen salesmen on the road combined. At the same time our salesmen increased their sales by having new features to talk. Thus Bissell carpet sweepers attained the position which they hold today. They came to control some 95 per cent of the trade. The advertising was done by the dealer. The demand grew and grew until the Bissell Company became, I believe, the richest concern in Grand Rapids.

My business was to devise three selling schemes a year. They all referred to finishes and woods. I found a man, for instance, who had patented a method of coloring veneers. The coloring liquid was placed on the under side. It came through the veneer wherever the ends of the grains showed on top, creating a weird and beautiful effect. I gave the resulting wood a coined name and inclosed samples in my letters.

Again I offered to supply dealers three gold-plated sweepers as a part of each dozen, exactly the same as we exhibited at the World's Fair in Chicago. Thus I placed thousands of World's Fair exhibits in windows the country over.

But in two or three years I found myself running out of schemes. There are distinct limitations to exciting varieties in carpet sweeper finishes.

New ideas came harder and harder. I felt that I was nearing the end of my resources, so I began to look for wider fields.

Just at that time Lord & Thomas of Chicago first offered me a position. They had a scheme man named Carl Greig, who was leaving them to go with the *Inter Ocean* to increase the circulation. Lord & Thomas, who had watched my sweeper-selling schemes, offered me his place. The salary was much higher than I received in Grand Rapids, so I told the Bissell people that I intended to take it. They called a directors' meeting. Every person on the board had, in times past, been my vigorous opponent. All had fought me tooth and nail on every scheme proposed. They had never ceased to ridicule my idea of talking woods in a machine for sweeping carpets. But they voted unanimously to meet the Lord & Thomas offer, so I stayed.

That, however, as I knew then, was but a temporary decision. I felt the call to a wider field, and the Chicago offer had whetted my ambitions. Soon after I received another and a larger offer, and resigned.

Chapter Five

Larger
fields

N ow I approach a tragic epoch in my life. I
was close to my limits in Grand Rapids. The
offer from Lord & Thomas gave me wider recogni-
tion. Ambition surged within me, because of my
mother's blood. I became anxious to go higher.

But I had built a new home in Grand Rapids.
All the friends I knew were about me. There I enjoyed prestige. I knew that in a larger field I would
have to sacrifice the things that I loved most.

I suppose I was right in my desires, according
to general standards. Ambition is everywhere ap-
plauded. But I have often returned to Grand Rapids to envy my old associates. They continued in
a quiet, sheltered field. They met no large demands. Success and money came to them in moderation. But in my turbulent life, as I review it, I

have found no joys they missed. Fame came to me, but I did not enjoy it. Money came in a measure, but I could never spend it with pleasure. My real inclination has always been toward the quiet paths. This story is written in gardens near Grand Rapids, where the homing instinct brought me. When my old friends and I get together here, it is hard to decide who took the wiser course.

Swift & Company, packers of Chicago, advertised for an advertising manager. I looked them up, and I found that their capital at that time was $15,000,000. I inquired about them, and I learned that they intended to spend $300,000 per year. That would place them at that time among the largest American advertisers. I could not see in the Bissell line one-tenth the chance they offered. So I resolved to obtain that Chicago position. I had no doubt of my ability to do so. In my Michigan field I was king, and I never dreamed that other potentates might treat me as a slave.

I went to Chicago, then out to the stockyards, and was referred to Mr. I. H. Rich. He was head of the butterine department and the man who had urged them to advertise.

"Mr. Rich," I said, "I have come for that position."

He smiled at me benevolently and asked for my name and address. Then he wrote my name down on a sheet which held many names before mine.

"What are all those names?" I asked.

"Why, they are other applicants!" said Mr. Rich. "There are one hundred and five of them. Your number is one hundred and six."

I was astounded. One hundred and six men considered themselves fitted for that high position. What effrontery!

I turned to Mr. Rich and said: "I came here mainly to learn where I stood in advertising. I did not really desire this position. My heart is in Grand Rapids, and I feel that my happiness lies there. But this is a challenge. I am going to prove myself best fitted for this place."

Mr. Rich smiled and said: "Go ahead, and God bless you. We are waiting to be convinced." Then after a brief talk he dismissed me.

I knew all of the leading advertising agents of Chicago. They had solicited my business. So that afternoon I went to each and said, "Please write today to I. H. Rich, care Swift & Company, Union Stockyards, Chicago, and say what you think of Claude Hopkins." All promised to do that, and I knew that some of them would write very flattering things.

That night I returned to Grand Rapids. It happened that I had lately been employed there by the Board of Trade to write a history of Grand Rapids. The members were delighted with it. Writing that book had brought me into contact with all the leading business men. I started out the next morning to see them. First I called on the bankers, then on the furniture-makers, then on the wholesalers, then on other business men. I spent several days in this quest. To each one I said, "Please write to I. H. Rich, care Swift & Company, Union Stock Yards, Chicago, and say what you think of Claude Hopkins as a writer and an advertising man." That started a flood of letters.

Then I went to the Grand Rapids *Herald* and said: "I want to write for you a daily two-column article on advertising. It will cost you nothing and it will educate your advertisers. All I ask is that you let me sign the articles and that you publish my picture in them."

They agreed, so every evening after office hours I wrote that two-column article. Then I took it to the office on my bicycle to reach the paper before midnight. Every article was addressed in reality to Swift & Company, to Mr. I. H. Rich. It was written to show what I knew about advertising. As the articles appeared I mailed them to Mr. Rich.

After three weeks of that daily bombardment I received a telegram from Swift & Company asking me to come to Chicago. I went, but with little idea of accepting the position. I had come to realize more than ever that I would be lonesome away from Grand Rapids. But I had to complete my conquest, so I went.

We had not discussed salary—that was too remote. So my idea of escape was to ask a salary

higher than they would pay. I did so, and Mr. L.
F. Swift, now president of the company, refused to
consider it. He had read none of my letters or articles. I had made no impression on him; all he
considered was my salary demand.

Mr. Rich then asked for another conference in
the afternoon, and took me out to lunch. At the
table he talked like a father. He pointed out the
narrow sphere I had, and always would have,
where I was. Swift & Company were offering me
one of the greatest positions in my line. They had
a score of lines to advertise. There I would have an
unlimited scope. He pictured the folly of refusing
such an opportunity, and I yielded to his persua-
sions. After lunch I went back and accepted the
salary offered, promising to start in three weeks.

The next morning in Grand Rapids I went up to
my home and saw the family on the porch. There
were shade trees in front and many flowers in the
yard. I contrasted that setting with the stockyards,
where the outlook covered only dirty pens filled
with cattle and hogs. The way to the office led
through a half-mile of mud. Then I regretted my
action. The price seemed too great to pay. Had
I not given my word I would have turned back
that morning to quiet insignificance. And now,
after looking back thirty years, I think I would
turn back this morning.

In three weeks I went to Chicago. I secured a
room on Forty-third Street, because the cars there

ran to the stockyards. The room was a small one, dark and dingy. I had to climb over my trunk to get into bed. On the dresser I placed a picture of my home in Grand Rapids, but I had to turn that picture to the wall before I could go to sleep.

The next morning I went to the stockyards and presented myself for work. Mr. Rich was away, so I was referred to Mr. L. F. Swift, now president of the company. He did not remember me.

I said, "Three weeks ago you employed me as advertising manager."

"Is that so?" he replied. "I had entirely forgotten. If you are really employed here, go out and talk with Howes."

Consider that reception for a lonely man, already half discouraged. For a proud man, who considered himself important. For a man from a small city where everybody knew him, his importance and his place.

But I was more unwelcome than I supposed. Mr. G. F. Swift, then head of the company, was in Europe when I was employed. It was his first vacation, and he could not endure it, so he hurried back. At once he asked what I was doing in his office. When told that I was there to spend his money, he took an intense dislike to me, and it never changed.

He set out at once to make my position untenable. The business he headed had been built without the use of print. He catered to nobody, asked nobody's patronage. He had gained what he could by sheer force. He had the same contempt for an advertising man that a general must have for a poet.

He made my way very hard. I had come from gentle surroundings, from an office filled with friends. There I entered the atmosphere of war. There every conception of business was conflict, inside and outside the office. We have nothing left in big business today to compare with the packing business of thirty years ago.

Mr. G. F. Swift was a deeply religious man. I am sure he did the right as he knew it. But he was an autocrat in the days when business was much like war. No one gave quarter or asked it. That was the attitude which later brought business into bad repute.

Mr. Swift was a fighter, and I became one of his targets. I typified a foolish outgo. I had been installed in his absence to waste his hard-earned money. So I suffered the consequences. Among the many who trembled at his word, I always trembled most.

Mr. Swift's conception of advertising referred in particular to signs on refrigerator cars. They went everywhere. Good advertising there consisted of light letters. I could never get them light enough.

Next came the annual calendars. He had very decided ideas about them, and they never agreed with mine. Nor could I carry out his ideas to his satisfaction.

One day he asked me to photograph a side of beef for hanging in his beef houses. I recognized this as a crucial test, so I called in a half-dozen photographers. The best sides of beef in storage were brought out for photographing. The next morning I sent him some dozens of pictures and asked him to make his choice.

Soon I saw Mr. Swift charging from his office, with his arms full of photographs, like a mad bull. He started for my desk, but stopped some twenty feet away and threw the pictures at me.

Then he came up and said: "Do you think that those things look like sides of beef? Where are the colors in them? Do you think that anybody wants black beef?"

I explained that photography could not show colors. Then he said, "I know a girl who can paint beef in colors. I will take my job to her." Thereafter that girl held a place in our office much better than mine.

The chief advertising project of Swift & Company in those days was Cotosuet. The N. K. Fairbank Company were advertising Cottolene, and making considerable strides. My chief problem in those days was to fight that competition.

Cottolene and Cotosuet were both brands of compound lard. They consisted of a mixture of cottonseed oil and beef suet. They were offered as substitutes for lard, and for butter in cooking, at a much lower price.

Cottolene, being the original product, had attained a big start and advantage. But it was expected that I, as an advertising man, could quickly overtake and defeat it. It was something like combating Ivory Soap with another white soap today.

We opened a sales office in Boston and started advertising in New England. We had hardly started when Mr. L. F. Swift came to my desk one day. He said: "Father is very nervous about this money spent in advertising. He considers it an utter waste. The results so far are not very encouraging. You have been here nearly six weeks, but our sales on Cotosuet have hardly increased at all."

I had no need to explain to him. He knew that advertising had hardly started. But I saw that I had to help him out by making some quick showing.

That night after dinner I paced the streets. I tried to analyze myself. I had made a great success in Grand Rapids; I was making a fizzle here. What were the reasons? What was there I did in the old field which I could apply to Swift & Company's problems?

At midnight, on Indiana Avenue, I thought of an idea. In Grand Rapids I created sensations, I presented enticing ideas. I did not say to people, "Buy my brand instead of the other fellow's." I offered them inducements which naturally led them to buy.

Why not apply those principles to Cotosuet? Rothschild & Company were then completing a new store. They would have an opening in two weeks. I knew Charles Jones, the advertising manager, and I decided to go to him and offer a sensation for his opening.

The next day I did so. His grocery department was on the fifth floor and it included a large bay window. I urged him to let me have that window for a unique exhibit. "I will build there," I said, "the largest cake in the world. I will advertise the cake in a big way in the newspapers. I will make that," I promised, "the greatest feature in your opening."

My idea was to make a cake with Cotosuet in place of butter. Then to argue that a product better than butter was certainly better than lard.

Mr. Jones accepted my proposition. Then I went next door to H. H. Kohlsaat & Co., bakers, and asked them to bake the cake. I told them to make the special tins which were necessary, to decorate the cake in a magnificent way, and to build it as high as the room. They did so.

At the time of the opening I inserted half-page ads. in the newspapers announcing the biggest cake in the world. That was on Saturday, and that night the store was to open. After dinner I started down to see the cake myself, but the cars stopped on State Street long before they reached the store. I stepped out and saw before me a perfect sea of people. After a long time of struggle I reached the doors. At every door I found a policeman. The authorities had closed the doors because the crowd was too large to admit.

During the next week, 105,000 people climbed four flights of stairs to that cake. The elevators could not carry them. There I had demonstrators to offer samples of the cake. Then we had prizes to offer to those who guessed nearest to the weight, but every guesser had to buy a pail of Cotosuet.

As a result of that week, Cotosuet was placed on a profit-paying basis in Chicago. We gained many thousands of users.

Then I organized a group to carry our plan through the Eastern states. The group consisted of a baker and decorator, three demonstrators and myself. We went to Boston and arranged an exhibit at the store of Cobb, Bates & Yerxa, but they threw us out the first forenoon. The crowd was so great that it destroyed all their chance to do business.

We went along the New York Central, and in every city we learned new ways to increase the results of our efforts. We went to the leading baker and showed him newspaper clippings of what we had done elsewhere. We offered to let him build the cake, and be advertised as its creator, on condition that he bought a carload of Cotosuet. Sometimes two carloads. We went to the leading grocery and proved the results of our cake-show. Then we offered to place the cake in his store if he ordered a carload in tins.

Wherever we went we sold enough Cotosuet to insure us a profit in advance. Then we hired boys on Main Street to cry out with their papers, "*Evening News. All about the Big Cake.*" As a result, we mobbed the stores where the cake was on display. And in every city we established thousands of regular users.

At last we came to Cleveland, where they had a public market. We could not there sell a carload to a grocer. But we arranged with the market to give us their band for a week, also their newspaper space. As a result, half the policemen in Cleveland were called there to keep the crowd moving. Ropes were stretched through the market. I doubt if the stalls sold much that week, but we certainly sold Cotosuet.

When I returned to Chicago, Mr. L. F. Swift said: "That is the greatest advertising stunt I have ever known. You have made good, both with father and with me."

Thus I won out with Swift & Company.

That, many say, was not advertising. Advertising to them is placing some dignified phrases in print. But commonplace dignity doesn't get far. Study salesmen, canvassers, and fakers if you want to know how to sell goods. No argument in the world can ever compare with one dramatic demonstration.

I have no sympathy with those who feel that fine language is going to sell goods at a profit. I have listened to their arguments for hours. They might as well say that full dress is an excellent diving suit. No dilettantes have any chance in prying money out of pockets. The way to sell goods is to sell them. The way to do that is to sample and demonstrate, and the more attractive you can make your demonstration the better it will be for you. The men who succeed in advertising are not the highly-bred, not the men careful to be unobtrusive and polite, but the men who know what arouses enthusiasm in simple people. The difference is the difference between Charlie Chaplin and Robert Mantell, or "After the Ball" and "The Moonlight Sonata." If we are going to sell, we must cater to the millions who buy.

Chapter Six

Personal
salesmanship

Despite my success, there came a time with Swift & Company when my advertising appeal lost all its persuasiveness. Cottolene cut prices. One of our largest fields was with bakers. They knew Cotosuet to be identical with Cottolene, and they refused to pay a higher price.

Swift & Company's business had been founded and developed on competition. They met any price that was offered. So they could not conceive of a product of theirs demanding a price above market.

I had fixed a price on Cotosuet one-half cent a pound above Cottolene. That price was essential to profit. I could obtain it from consumers, but the bakery trade formed a large part of our business. We had a branch office in Boston, for instance, costing $2,000 per month. Six salesmen went out from there, and Mr. Aldrich was in charge. We gave them little credit for sales made to grocers, as a result of the demand we created. And their sales to bakers, at our higher price, became almost *nil*.

One day Mr. Swift called me to his office. He said: "Here is a letter from Boston. I agree with it entirely. They are not making sales, and they cannot make sales, at the price you have fixed on our product."

"They are wrong," I replied. "Real salesmanship has no regard for price. I am selling to consumers at our over-price. Why can't they sell to bakers?"

Mr. Swift said: "Can you do it?"

I replied that I could. I could sell to bakers just as well as consumers on the principles I advised.

"Then," he asked, "when can you go to Boston?"

"I can go in two weeks," I said. "I have much work to clean up."

"Can you go this afternoon?" he asked. "This is an urgent matter. We are losing much money in Boston. I want to know the right and wrong before we go much farther."

"I will go this afternoon," I said. I walked out to my desk and found it piled high with important matters. I told my assistant to care for them. Then I picked up the proof of a street-car card which had just been submitted—a picture of a pie—and placed it under my arm.

When I arrived in Boston I met Mr. Aldrich, discouraged and cynical. He told me what he had told Mr. Swift. I was a theorist in business. No one could hope to sell Cotosuet at a price above Cottolene, and no salesman did.

I said, "Tell me some one you can't sell."

Mr. Aldrich replied: "They are all about us. We can't sell anyone."

"Tell me one concern," I said.

"Well, take the Fox Pie Company of Chelsea," he replied. "They are the largest around us."

"Lead me at once to them," I said.

Mr. Aldrich did so. When we arrived we found Mr. Fox in his shirt sleeves in the bakery. We waited for him awhile.

When he came up to greet us I found him in a rather cantankerous mood. He was busy and he knew we had nothing he desired. So he decided to dispose of us, as I saw, in short order.

But I greeted him like a contemporary. I said: "I am advertising manager of Swift & Company. I have come from Chicago to consult you about a card."

I placed the card some fifty feet away, then I stepped back and asked him to regard it.

"That card," I said, "is intended to picture the ideal pie. It has cost us a great deal of money. The artist charged us $250 for the drawing. Then it has to be engraved on stone. Those colors you see there are produced by twelve separate printings on stone." I explained the process as well as I knew it. And, being different from baking, he was interested in it.

I told him that before printing those cards I wanted to obtain his approval. And I did. He was a pie expert, and I wanted his ideas on that pie.

Instantly he changed from baker to a critic. We began to discuss that pie card. When I found fault with any feature, he defended it. Never before, in all probability, had he been asked to appear in the role of adviser. He, like all of us, enjoyed the new situation.

Finally he insisted that the pie card represented a pie at its best. Nothing could be done to improve it. He would have the whole trade of Boston if he could make pies like that.

Then I urged him to have it. I said: "How many stores in Boston are selling Fox Pies?"

"About one thousand," he replied.

I said: "I will furnish you a card like that to go in every store. You have been good to me. Let me do something to reciprocate. I must advertise Cotosuet on those cards. Let me say on each that nothing but Swift's Cotosuet is used in the shortening for Fox's pies. I will furnish you 250 of those cards with every car load of Cotosuet that you order now."

He accepted that offer and ordered four carloads to get one thousand cards.

Then I went to Providence, and at Altman's bakery made the same arrangement. Then to New Haven, then Hartford, Springfield, and all big New England cities. In not one did I fail to sell the leading baker a large supply of Cotosuet. He paid a higher price than for Cottolene, but he secured a great advantage.

I returned to Boston with more orders for Cotosuet than six salesmen had sold in six weeks. But Mr. Aldrich was scornful.

"You have not been selling Cotosuet," he said. "You have simply sold a pie card. Now let me see what you can do where you have no such advantage. One of our largest customers is Mansfield Baking Company, Springfield, Mass. There you have given exclusive rights to your pie card. I would like to see what you can do with ordinary salesmanship."

I went at once to Springfield, and reached there late Saturday afternoon. I went to the Mansfield bakery, and found Teddy Mansfield in his shirt sleeves, working. I waited until he was done. Then I said: "Teddy, I have an invitation to the Commercial Club banquet tonight. I am lonesome and I don't want to go alone. They will let me bring a guest. I want you to go with me."

Teddy rebelled. He said he had never been to a banquet. He had no suitable clothes. I told him that I was wearing just what I had on then. So he finally consented.

That was a great night for Teddy Mansfield. He met for the first time with the leading men of his city. He enjoyed himself, and when we parted he was very friendly to me.

That night at the hotel door I said: "I am coming to see you Monday morning to present something of great interest to you."

"Please don't come," he said. "You have been so kind tonight that I can't refuse you anything. But I am loaded with Cotosuet. I have forty tierces in my cellar, and I cannot afford to use them, as you know. I shall be glad to see you, but don't ask me to buy Cotosuet."

On Monday morning I found Teddy Mansfield, as usual, in his shirt sleeves. I said: "Teddy, I don't want to talk Cotosuet to you, but I have a proposition. I am advertising manager of Swift & Company. I can do in some ways what no one else can do. You are known in Springfield, but nobody knows you outside. I want to suggest a way to advertise Mansfield's pies all the way from here to Chicago."

Then I unfolded my plan. If he would order two carloads of Cotosuet, I would place a sign on both sides of the cars. That sign would announce that all that Cotosuet was to be used in Mansfield's pies in Springfield, Mass. "Not on one side of the car," I said, "but on both sides, so everyone for nine hundred miles, on both sides of the tracks, will know you."

That idea appealed to Teddy, as like ideas have appealed to countless advertisers before and since. It was folly, some say, but no more folly than all the ideas of "keeping your name before the people." Teddy typified the average advertiser of those days, in his desire simply to spread his fame. He accepted my offer, and in one week the cars arrived. I was there to greet them with him. I have rarely seen a man so pleased as was Teddy Mansfield when he saw those cars with signs which had advertised Mansfield's pies all the nine hundred miles from Chicago.

I had sold more Cotosuet in one week than six salesmen had sold in six weeks. Not one buyer had complained about the price. Mr. Swift wired me to fire the whole Boston force, but I asked him to wait until I returned and explained my methods to him.

When I met Mr. Swift I said: "I did not sell Cotosuet, did not talk Cotosuet. I sold pie cards and schemes, and Cotosuet went with them."

"Then I wish you would teach our other men to do that."

"It cannot be taught," I replied. And I am still of that opinion. The difference lies in the basic conception of selling. The average salesman openly seeks favors, seeks profit for himself. His plea is, "Buy my goods, not the other fellow's." He makes a selfish appeal to selfish people, and of course he meets resistance.

I was selling service. The whole basis of my talk was to help the baker get more business. The advantage to myself was covered up in my efforts to please him.

I have always applied that same principle to advertising. I never ask people to buy. I rarely even say that my goods are sold by dealers, I seldom quote a price. The ads. all offer service, perhaps a free sample or a free package. They sound altruistic. But they get a reading and get action from people seeking to serve themselves. No selfish appeal can do that.

Today that same principle is widely applied to house-to-house canvassing. Sellers of brushes call to offer the housewife a brush as a gift. Sellers of aluminum ware present a dish. Sellers of coffee call at first with a half-pound free package to try. They are always welcome. The housewife is all smiles and attention. Then, in the natural reaction, she strives to find a way to reciprocate the courtesy by buying.

Makers of vacuum sweepers offer to send one for a week's use in housecleaning. Makers of electric motors offer to send one to run the sewing-machine or the fan for a week. Cigar-makers send out boxes of cigars to anyone who asks. They say: "Smoke ten, then return the balance if you desire. The test will cost you nothing." All sorts of things are sent on approval. Nearly everything sold is sold subject to return. All good salesmanship, in print or in person, is based on some appealing service.

Good salesmen study to make their appeals inviting. One says: "Send me the money and I will return it if the article is not satisfactory." Another says: "Send no money. Let me send the article for trial, then remit or return it, just as you desire."

I buy many books by mail. In nearly every issue of certain magazines I see descriptions of books I may want. The ads. do not say, "Send the money." If they did my purchases would be few. My check book is at the office. By the next day, in all probability, the book would be forgotten. But they offer to send me the book to examine. I simply mail the coupon. I tear it out at once, put it in my pocket, and mail it the next morning.

In my early years in advertising those ideas of salesmanship were new. I was, I believe, among the first to apply them. No doubt I originated many of their applications. I never tried to sell anything, even in my retail-store advertising. I always offered a favor. Now I talk of service, profit, pleasure, gifts, not any desires of my own.

The house-to-house canvasser must apply those principles, else his sales are limited. So must the mail-order advertiser, whose results are known. But the advertiser who proceeds without knowing results often ignores these principles. Everywhere we see advertisers merely crying a name. They say: "Buy my brand. Be sure to get the original." Their whole evident desire is some selfish advantage. Such advertising may sometimes pay to an extent, but it never can pay like appeals which appear unselfish.

But Swift & Company refused to give anything away. I could never sample their products. We advertised wool soap, washing powder, breakfast sausage, hams and bacon and butterine, and we were reasonably successful. But I came to realize that under their restrictions any real success was impossible. All the years since have confirmed my opinion. The packers make many lines which can be profitably advertised. But I do not know of an advertising success made by a packing house, with the possible exception of Cudahy's Dutch Cleanser. There were special reasons for that. All their advertising opportunities have been lost through selfishness. They were bred in the idea that business is a fight, that sales must be forced, that competition must be undersold. Those ideas have been modified materially, but never so much as to make any packer an advertiser. That is, no advertising success in the packing line that I know of matches the opportunity.

In my day in the stockyards, about all my conceptions of selling in print were taboo. I saw that I had to escape those restrictions to accomplish my ambitions. So I began to look about.

Chapter Seven

Medical
advertising

Now I come to a class of advertising of which I no longer approve. Thirty years ago, medicine advertising offered the ad.-writer his greatest opportunity. It formed the supreme test of his skill. Medicines were worthless merchandise until a demand was created. They could not well be inventoried on the druggists' shelves at even one cent a bottle. Everything depended on the advertising.

The test of an ad.-writer in medicine advertising was as severe as in mail-order advertising today. He was shown up quickly by the item of profit and loss. Either he sold the goods at a profit or he did not. Salesmen, dealers, or clerks could not help him. One may sell flour, oatmeal, or soap by loading a dealer up or by offering inducements. Many things may contribute in selling a staple. It is sometimes hard to measure just what advertising does. Not so in a medicine. Advertising must do all.

Because of that fact, the greatest advertising men of my day were schooled in the medicine field. All of them have graduated. But all of them realize that medical advertising placed men on their mettle. It weeded out the incompetents, and gave scope and prestige to those who survived, as few other lines have done. The only lines today which so try men in the fire are some forms of mail-order advertising.

Medicines in those days dominated the advertising field. The best magazines accepted them. Almost nobody questioned their legitimacy. No more than they questioned railroad rebates, or passes to employees, in my packing-house experience. We must remember, in reviewing medicine advertising, how experience and education changes ideas and principles.

Every evil of the past had its logical defense. The medicine-makers included many high-minded men. They felt that they were serving humanity by offering good remedies for common conditions at very modest cost. They were aiding those who could not afford physicians. There was much reason in their arguments. Every medicine-maker received thousands of testimonials. And I still believe that those medicine-makers did far more good than harm. Even though the good came largely through mental impressions.

But medical science advanced. Doctors themselves turned largely away from drugs. We came to realize that ailing people should have a diagnosis. The real trouble should be located, instead of quelling symptoms. In a large percentage of cases it was unwise to advise self-medication.

I came to that conclusion many years ago. I have not advertised a medicine, save for simple ailments, for seventeen years or over. I would not do so under any circumstances. Just as I write this, I am refusing an appropriation of $900,000 to advertise a medicine. I stand as strongly as anyone today against advertising anything which opposes public good as we see it now.

So please remember that what I recite here occurred many years ago. It accorded with existing principles and practices. I have never known higher minded men than those who engaged in these enterprises. I am dealing with advertising as it applies to all conditions and all times. What should be advertised for the common good forms an entirely different question.

While with Swift & Company I wrote an article on patent-medicine advertising. It reached the attention of Dr. Shoop in Racine, Wisconsin. He was selling medicines through agents. He had no drug-store trade. The agency business was dying, so he was seeking a way to place his line on the drug-store shelves. He wrote me to come and see him.

I was discouraged with food products advertised under packing-house restrictions. I knew that medicine offered the greatest opportunity to an advertising man. So I went to Racine, talked with Dr. Shoop, and finally accepted what he offered.

I found a line of remedies sold through agents only. Not a bottle was in drug stores. The ordinary agent could not survive, so the business was dying fast. My duty was to create a demand which would bring the sales to drug stores. Not one man in a million could have met that test without the experience in retail selling which I had attained.

Night after night Dr. Shoop and I discussed the situation. I told him all I had done by talking ideas not connected with the product. Then we evolved the idea of a druggist's signed guaranty. People were not buying medicine, they were buying results. Many an advertiser a thousand miles away offered to guarantee results, but the guarantors were strangers. I conceived the idea of having a neighborhood druggist, to whom people paid their money, sign the guaranty.

First I tried this plan out on a cough cure. It brought enormous results. Here was one cough cure which anyone could buy without risk. If it brought the results we promised, it was worth many times its cost. If it failed, it was free. No cough cure on the market then could compete with that.

Later I tested the same plan on other remedies—on Dr. Shoop's Restorative, on his Rheumatic

Cure. It worked like magic. Others made claims, but we offered a certainty. And we secured most of the trade.

Our guaranties were based on a purchase of six bottles for five dollars. Few users purchased that amount. But the guaranty gave them confidence in every one-bottle purchase. Nobody in our field had any chance to compete with us.

We were very cautious in those days. We did not venture into newspaper advertising. We distributed books from house to house in cities of over 1,500 population. We secured mailing lists of heads of families in every village or hamlet below that. Those were the days before rural delivery. I had complete mailing lists of all heads of families in some 86,000 post offices of the United States and Canada.

The methods we used then have little interest now. Conditions have changed. We have learned that newspapers offer the cheapest distribution of any offer we wish to make. But for years we mailed and distributed some 400,000 books per day.

Later we graduated from that and got into the newspapers. We secured results at one-third our former cost. We came to spend $400,000 per year in newspaper advertising, and the results at that time made me the leader in proprietary advertising.

What I wish to emphasize here is that my proposals were always altruistic. I was always offering service. Anyone could try what I offered without risk. It either brought results beyond what I promised or the cost was *nil*. There was nothing in the field in those days to match any offer like that.

In advertising and merchandising, that is something always to consider. One must outbid all others in some way. He must offer advantages in qualities, service, or terms, or he must create a seeming advantage by citing facts which others fail to cite. Crying a name or brand is not sufficient. Urging people to buy from you instead of others goes against the grain. One must know his competition, know what others offer, know what people want. Until one feels sure that the advantages are strongly on his side, it is folly to risk a battle. One cannot long fool people who are carefully spending money. Never pay the price to get them unless you see clearly how you can keep them. Don't under-estimate the intelligence and the information of people who count their pennies.

I spent six and one-half years in Racine. Office hours began at seven o'clock in the morning. We knew that extra hours gave us an extra advantage. And we were competing in one of the hardest fields that advertising ever knew.

But my day never ended at the office. I had a typewriter in my home. I considered medicine as but one item, though a supreme test of advertising skill. So I devoted the rest of my waking hours to outside enterprises.

The J. L. Stack Advertising Agency handled the Dr. Shoop advertising. I arranged with them to write all of their advertising. Racine was a manufacturing center. So I set out to develop, after office hours, advertising enterprises there. And from each I learned a great deal.

One of the clients of J. L. Stack was Montgomery, Ward & Co. I wrote and directed their advertising. Many new merchandising plans were inaugurated. My everlasting argument was against dealing with people in the mass. For instance, a woman wrote in about a sewing-machine. She had that, and nothing else, on her mind. The general plan then was to send a catalog, treating all inquiries alike. I urged that every inquirer should be treated like a prospect who came to a store. We had a special catalog on sewing-machines, showing every style and price. We sent every inquirer the names of all in her vicinity who had bought our sewing-machines. We asked her to see the machines and to talk with their owners.

There I learned another valuable principle in advertising. In a wide-reaching campaign we are too apt to regard people in the mass. We try to broadcast our seed in the hope that some part will take root. That is too wasteful to ever bring a profit. We must get down to individuals. We must treat people in advertising as we treat them in person. Center on their desires. Consider the person who stands before you with certain expressed desires. However big your business, get down to the units, for those units are all that make size.

Schlitz Beer was another advertising campaign which I handled for J. L. Stack. Schlitz was then in fifth place. All brewers at that time were crying "Pure." They put the word "Pure" in large letters. Then they took double pages to put it in larger letters. The claim made about as much impression on people as water makes on a duck.

I went to a brewing school to learn the science of brewing, but that helped me not at all. Then I went through the brewery. I saw plate-glass rooms where beer was dripping over pipes, and I asked the reason for them. They told me those rooms were filled with filtered air, so the beer could be cooled in purity. I saw great filters filled with white-wood pulp. They explained how that filtered the beer. They showed how they cleaned every pump and pipe, twice daily, to avoid contaminations. How every bottle was cleaned four times by machinery. They showed me artesian wells, where they went 4,000 feet deep for pure water, though their brewery was on Lake Michigan. They showed me the vats where beer was aged for six months before it went out to the user.

They took me to their laboratory and showed me their original mother yeast cell. It had been developed by 1,200 experiments to bring out the utmost in flavor. All of the yeast used in making Schlitz Beer was developed from that original cell.

I came back to the office amazed. I said: "Why don't you tell people these things? Why do you merely try to cry louder than others that your beer is pure? Why don't you tell the reasons?"

"Why," they said, "the processes we use are just the same as others use. No one can make good beer without them."

"But," I replied, "others have never told this story. It amazes everyone who goes through your brewery. It will startle everyone in print."

So I pictured in print those plate-glass rooms and every other factor in purity. I told a story common to all good brewers, but a story which had never been told. I gave purity a meaning. Schlitz jumped from fifth place to neck-and-neck with first place in a very few months. That campaign remains to this day one of my greatest accomplishments. But it also gave me the basis for many another campaign. Again and again I have told simple facts, common to all makers in the line—too common to be told. But they have given the article first allied with them an exclusive and lasting prestige.

That situation occurs in many, many lines. The maker is too close to his product. He sees in his methods only the ordinary. He does not realize that the world at large might marvel at those methods, and that facts which seem commonplace to him might give him vast distinction.

That is a situation which occurs in most advertising problems. The article is not unique. It embodies no great advantages. Perhaps countless people can make similar products. But tell the pains you take to excel. Tell factors and features which others deem too commonplace to claim. Your product will come to typify those excellencies. If others claim them afterward, it will only serve to advertise you. There are few advertised products which cannot be imitated. Few who dominate a field have any exclusive advantage. They were simply the first to tell certain convincing facts.

Mr. Cyrus W. Curtis, of the Curtis Publishing Company, told me an interesting incident connected with that Schlitz campaign. He had never drunk beer, had never admitted the word beer or wine to the columns of the *Ladies' Home Journal.* But he took into the diner on a train a copy of *Life* containing one of these Schlitz ads. The ad. so impressed him that he ordered a bottle of Schlitz. He wanted to taste a product made under such purity ideals.

Among my friends in Racine was Jim Rohan. He was a clerk on small salary. He was in love with a school-teacher whom his salary did not permit him to marry. But he had an idea about incubators. And he felt that exploitation of that idea would give him money enough to marry.

I told him that I would exploit the idea, and I did. I read something like seventy-five incubator catalogs and ads. They were much alike. All the makers were fawning salesmen trying to urge a preference. I analyzed the situation and tried to find a unique method of attack.

I found a practical chicken-raiser, and I asked permission to write a book in his name. He was an independent fellow who cared nothing for mere opinions. So I characterized him in my book. Writing in this man's name, and on facts which he gave me, I asked nobody to buy Racine Incubators. I simply told his experience. He had tried all sorts of incubators, and he knew their fallacious claims. He had settled down to practical money-making, and these were the methods he used. He would help and encourage those who wished to follow him, but he had no sympathy for those who followed every will-o'-the-wisp.

That plea proved a winner. Most seekers after incubators wrote for five or six catalogs. They all read alike, except mine. Here was a rugged and practical man who cared more for serving than selling, and the practical people who were seeking for profit naturally followed him.

But Racine Incubators were high-priced. A great many converts paused when they compared the lower prices offered. So I urged Mr. Rohan to start another company, called the Belle City Incubator Company, and there to offer incubators at much lower prices on other inducements.

We followed up inquiries on the Racine line for ten days. Then, when we saw too great a resistance, we offered the Belle City line. Thus we secured a double chance on incubator buyers. Otherwise, with our best efforts, we could never have earned a profit. As it was, we built a business which today is quite extensive. And I know of no rival of the old times who survived.

We organized and advertised numerous other lines in Racine. One was the Racine Bath Cabinet, one was Racine Refrigerators. Those were excellent advertising experiences, because there were no uncertainties, no repeats.

The Racine Shoe Company manufactured excellent shoes. They were in the center of the leather region between Chicago and Milwaukee. Their shoes at that time sold at an average of $2.15 per pair at wholesale. I organized what I called the "Racine Club." It sold Racine Shoes to club members only at advantageous prices. I quoted to club members $3 per pair delivered, and I offered the choice of six styles. The shoes cost me an average of $2.15 per pair. The average express rate was 35 cents per pair. So my clear average profit was 50 cents per pair. But a membership cost 25 cents, and no one could buy without having a membership. The cost of my advertising was paid by my membership fees. Then with each pair of shoes I sent twelve memberships with catalogs, etc. Anyone who sold those twelve memberships could obtain his shoes at 25 cents per pair. A membership entitled the bearer to buy a pair of shoes at $3, with twelve more certificates worth 25 cents each.

I was offering shoes at $3 which would cost $3.50 to $5 at the stores. But I offered them to a limited clientele. None but club members could buy them. Every buyer, if he chose, could sell the membership certificates at 25 cents each. If he did so, his shoes would cost him only 25 cents. When my advertising secured a few buyers, they became salesmen for me. So a little advertising created for me an overwhelming trade. It soon exceeded the capacity of the Racine Shoe Company, and orders were much delayed.

The fly in this ointment was the fact that shoes did not always fit, and I guaranteed a fit. The returns absorbed most of my profits. But I learned a new angle in selling. I learned how customers, whether in direct selling or otherwise, could influence future returns.

All that time I was continuing to advertise retail sales the country over. I experimented locally with every sort of sale. Whenever I found a plan which brought large returns, I told other dealers about it. This was all night work. I never thought of sleep. My whole ambition was to find ways to lead people to buy, and I found them in plenty. What I found then has been the foundation of all the success I have gained.

Chapter Eight

My Liquozone
experience

M y years in Racine gave me unique experience in advertising proprietaries, and brought me wide reputation. My methods were new. Testimonials had been almost universal in those lines. I published none. Reckless claims were common. My ads. said in effect, "Try this cough remedy; watch the benefits it brings. It cannot harm, for no opiates are in it. If it succeeds, the cough will stop. If it fails, it is free. Your own druggist signs the warrant."

The appeal was overwhelming, almost resistless. Ever since then my chief study has been to create appeals like that. When we make an offer one cannot reasonably refuse, it is pretty sure to gain acceptance. And however generous the offer, however open to imposition, experience proves that very few will cheat those who offer a square deal.

Try to hedge or protect yourself, and human nature likes to circumvent you. But remove all restrictions and say, "We trust you," and human nature likes to justify that trust. All my experience in advertising has shown that people in general are honest.

A certain man in Chicago had made a small fortune out of the Oliver typewriter, but the line was not to his liking. He was a natural advertiser, and had long been searching for the product.

While he was building a factory in Montreal, a number of men came to tell him of a germicide made in Toronto. It was called "Powley's Liquified Ozone." Many institutions in Canada were indorsing and employing it. And, without any advertising, countless people had learned of it and used it with remarkable results.

Finally this man was induced to go to Toronto to investigate the product. He found a gas-made germicide, harmless for internal use. He interviewed hundreds who had tried it, including hospitals and Catholic institutions, and became enthused.

He bought the product for $100,000, then changed the name to Liquozone. Then he started to advertise and market it. He sought out an able advertising man and made a year's contract with him. The next year he selected another man. In four years he tried out four advertising men who had convinced him of their ability, but the result was utter failure. All the money invested in the business had been dissipated. The company was heavily in debt. Its balance sheet showed a net worth of some $45,000 less than nothing. Which shows how rare is the experience and the ability to advertise a proprietary product.

Still this determined advertiser remained undiscouraged. He believed in his product, and he felt that some man somewhere knew how to make it win. He said, "We will try it one year more, and this time we'll find the man."

On the last day of the fourth year he called on all the leading advertising agents of Chicago, and he asked each one to name the best man they knew of for a product of that kind. As I was at that time the particular star in that field, I believe all of them named me.

His last call was on J. L. Stack, and he put the same question to him. Just then a telegram came in from me, accepting an invitation to dine with Mr. Stack that New-year's Eve. Mr. Stack showed the telegram and said: "That is the man, of course. No doubt others have told you. But his employer is my client. I can do nothing to harm his interests. Hopkins is my friend, and I never could advise him to consider your hopeless proposition."

The advertiser replied: "If Hopkins is the man you say, he can probably take care of himself. Let me dine with you tonight and meet him."

That was my first contact with Liquozone. Its promoter was a charming man. His powers of persuasion were almost resistless. So, against my wishes, he induced me to stay over and meet him the next day.

That was New-year's Day. I wanted to be at home. The Liquozone office where we met was a dingy affair. The floors and the desks were rough pine. The heat came from a rusty, round, wood-burning stove. The surroundings were disheartening, the company was bankrupt. I resented being kept in Chicago for New-year's Day on such a proposition. So our interview was neither pleasant nor encouraging.

But the man who could smile and start over, after four years of failure, was not to be blocked by my attitude. In a few days he followed me to Racine. Then he asked me to accompany him on a three-day trip to Toronto. I accepted for the pleasure of his company and because I wanted a vacation.

In Toronto he placed at my disposal a vehicle and a guide. For three days I visited institutions and people who had seen the results of Liquozone. I had never heard such stories as they told. At the end of the third day I said: "I have found here a still greater reason why I cannot join with you. I am not a big enough man to tell the world about that product. I cannot do it justice. So I beg you again to forget me."

But the man was not to be denied. In a few days he came again to Racine, and we discussed the project all night. At four o'clock in the morning, worn out by importunity, impressed by the argument of duty, I accepted his meager proposals.

I was to be given no salary, because there was no money to pay salaries. In lieu of that, I was to have a one-fourth interest in a bankrupt concern. I was to leave my beautiful offices and take a pine desk on Kinzie Street. I was to leave my friends and go out among strangers. I was to exchange my apartments in a hotel on Lake Michigan for a dingy $45-per-month flat in Chicago, where my wife had to do her own work. I was to walk to the office to save street-car fare, so my savings might be conserved. I had a steam automobile, the first in Racine and the joy of my leisure. I had to leave that.

Friends gave me farewell parties, but the conversation at all of them centered on my foolishness. A delegation was sent to ride with me to Chicago, and to argue against my folly all the way. My closest friend repudiated me entirely. He said that good sense was a prime requisite in a friend.

I am sure that few men ever entered a business adventure under darker skies. But I want to say here that every great accomplishment of my life has been won against such opposition. Every move that led upward, or to greater happiness or content, has been fought by every friend I had. Perhaps because they were selfish and wanted me to stay with them.

I have met other great emergencies, more important than money or business. I have always had to meet them alone. I have had to decide for myself, and always against tremendous opposition. Every great move I have made in life has been ridiculed and opposed by my friends. The greatest winnings I have made, in happiness, in money or content, have been accomplished amid almost universal scorn.

But I have reasoned in this way: The average man is not successful. We meet few who attain their goal, few who are really happy or content. Then why should we let the majority rule in matters affecting our lives?

Success has come to me in sufficient measure, happiness in abundance, and absolute content. Not one of those blessings would have come to me had I followed the advice of my friends.

As a result, I never give advice. We have our own lives to live, our own careers to make. We have no way of measuring others' desires and capacities. Some are weak. A discouraging word at a critical moment may change their entire course. Then the one who gives that word incurs the responsibility. I court no obligations of that kind. Advertising teaches us how fallible are our judgments, even in things we know best. We have nowhere near an even chance when we attempt to give advice.

I went into Liquozone under the circumstances stated. I was playing a desperate game. Four men in four years had failed utterly. Yet on this dubious venture I was staking all I had.

Night after night I paced Lincoln Park, trying to evolve a plan. I held to my old conceptions. Serve better than others, offer more than others, and you are pretty sure to win.

One morning I came to the office and said: "I have the winning idea. Let us buy the first fifty-cent bottle. Then, to all who accept, let us offer a guaranty on six dollar bottles. We pay for the first bottle. If that test leads one to continue, we take the risk on the rest."

My associate was appalled. He said: "We are bankrupt now. Your proposition will throw us into chaos."

But I obtained his permission to try my plan in a dozen small Illinois cities. We offered a fifty-cent bottle free. To each inquirer we sent an order on a certain local druggist for the bottle, and said, "We will pay the price."

Then we sent to each inquirer a guaranty offering six dollar bottles for five dollars. The druggist would sign the warrant. If results from those six bottles proved unsatisfactory, every penny would be returned.

Consider how irresistible was such a proposition. A fifty-cent bottle free. Then a five-dollar lot under warrant. "Just say to your druggist that you are dissatisfied, and your money will be returned without argument."

I had a proposition which no reasonable person could refuse. As most people are reasonable, I knew that most people in need would accept it. My offer was impregnable.

We found in those test cities that our inquiries for free bottles cost us 18 cents each. We waited thirty days, and we found that our sale was 90 cents per inquirer. The profit on our sales far more than paid the advertising before the bills were due. And the claims made under our guaranty amounted to less than 2 per cent on our sales.

I secured statements from the druggists advertised citing these results. Then I sent those statements to other leading druggists, one in each city. I also recited the results I had obtained for them in other proprietary lines. With each letter I inclosed a contract. It specified the advertising to be done. It promised that all inquiries for the free bottle would be referred one certain store. The condition was an order, the amount of which would more than cover that advertising. The order was a definite one for a product they had never seen. But we secured those orders from leading druggists—all by letter—to an amount exceeding $100,000. Then we took the orders to our advertising agent. We said: "We have no money. We owe you $16,000 which we cannot pay. But here are orders from good druggists for $100,000. Let us assign them to you for that amount of advertising. That is the only way, and a sure way, to get back what we owe you."

The agency accepted that proposition because they had no alternative. They had too little conception of proved advertising to realize our position. They ran the advertising, and the results came from everywhere, just as they did in our test towns. We received in the next year over 1,500,000 requests for the free bottle. The average cost per request was 18 cents, just as it was in our test cities. The average sale per request was 91 cents, or just a trifle more than in test cities.

I went with Liquozone in February. We had no money, save enough to pay our rent. In our first fiscal year, commencing July 1, our net profits were $1,800,000. The next year we invaded Europe. We established a London office where we employed 306 people. We built a factory in France, and fitted out one of the finest offices in Paris. In two years we were advertising in seventeen languages and were selling Liquozone in nearly every country of the world.

Germicides are uncertain propositions. New ones come to supplant the old. We recognized that, so we moved rapidly. In three years we bought for people nearly five million fifty-cent bottles. We made hay while the sun shone. But that Liquozone business still exists and it still is profitable.

What was the secret of that success? Just the daring which led me to abandon safety for uncertainty. Then to buy a fifty-cent bottle for everyone who sent a coupon. Then to guarantee results. We had confidence in our product, we had confidence in people. All the way along, every man consulted told us we were reckless. Every director, every adviser, quit us in disgust.

There are other ways, I know, to win in selling and in advertising. But they are slow and uncertain. Ask a person to take a chance on you, and you have a fight. Offer to take a chance on him, and the way is easy.

I have always taken chances on the other fellow. I have analyzed my proposition until I made sure that he had the best end of the bargain. Then I had something people could not well neglect.

I have been robbed in plenty, but the robbery cost me ten times less than trying to enforce any safe proposition. Now most leading merchants have come to the same conclusion. Anything bought in a leading store is subject to return. So with goods ordered by mail. And countless advertisers send out goods to strangers on approval. They say, "Try for ten days," or, "Examine these books," or, "Smoke ten of these cigars at our risk." The man who tries to play safety against this almost universal trend finds himself handicapped. And the cost of his sales is doubled or trebled, with the best that he can do.

Chapter Nine

The start
of my seventeen years
with an advertising agency

I spent five years with Liquozone—five stren-
uous years. I traveled from office to office, here
and abroad. Every country presented new problems.

One night in Paris I called in a famous doctor.
He told me I was a nervous wreck. He said, "The
only thing that can save you is to go home and
rest."

"I have no home," I said. "I live in a hotel.
This hotel is very much like it. I might as well
stay here."

But he insisted. Then I thought of a fruit farm
on Spring Lake, Michigan, which I had so often
plowed as a boy. I remembered one name there,
Robert Ferris. I had heard he had built a hotel.
So I cabled him for accommodations.

I received his reply in New York. The hotel had been torn down, but he had cottages neatly furnished with all one could desire. "All you need to bring is your trunk."

So I sent him a check for the cottage, and I came on with my trunk. For three months I basked in the sunshine, sleeping, playing, and drinking milk. Then I went to Chicago, fully resolved to give up those efforts which had wrecked me and to live the quiet life. I invited some friends to a luncheon to say farewell to business. I was the gayest of the gay. I intended to keep busy, but I would write in the future for fame and not for money.

At the second course a young man came to our table. He said, "Mr. A. D. Lasker of Lord & Thomas requests you to call on him this afternoon."

I knew what that meant. It meant a new career of serfdom, as I saw it. I was nervous, distracted, and ill. It meant night and day service to show others ways to make more money.

I turned to my friends at the table, and said: "Mr. Lasker cannot do this. I have played my part. I will go to see him because I respect him. But he can never induce me to enter the vortex of advertising again."

I kept the engagement. Mr. Lasker handed me a contract from the Van Camp Packing Company for $400,000. It was based on the condition that copy be submitted satisfactory to Mr. Van Camp.

Mr. Lasker said: "I have searched the country for copy. This is copy I got in New York, this in Philadelphia. I have spent thousands of dollars to get the best copy obtainable. You see the result. Neither you nor I would submit it. Now I ask you to help me. Give me three ads, which will start this campaign, and your wife may go down Michigan Avenue to select any car on the street and have it charged to me."

So far as I know, no ordinary human being has ever resisted Albert Lasker. He has commanded what he would in this world. Presidents have made him their pal. Nothing he desired has ever been forbidden him.

So I yielded, as all do, to his persuasiveness. I went to Indianapolis that night. The next day I started investigators to learn the situation in respect to pork and beans. I found that 94 per cent of the housewives baked their own pork and beans. Only 6 per cent were amenable to any canned-bean argument. Yet all the advertisers of pork and beans were merely crying, "Buy my brand."

I started a campaign to argue against home baking. Of course I offered samples of factory baking. I told of the sixteen hours required to bake beans at home. I told why home baking could never make beans digestible. I pictured home-baked beans, with the crisped beans on top, the mushy beans below. I told how we selected our beans, of the soft water we used, of our steam ovens where we baked beans for hours at 245 degrees. Then I offered a free sample for comparison. The result was an enormous success.

After a while, when others followed us, we suffered substitution. Our rivals tried to meet it by insisting on their brand. They said in effect, "Give me the money which you give to others." And such appeals fell on deaf ears.

I came out with headlines, "Try Our Rivals, Too." I urged people to buy the brands suggested and compare them with Van Camp's. That appeal won over others. If we were certain enough of our advantage to invite such comparisons, people were certain enough to buy.

That's another big point to consider. Argue anything for your own advantage, and people will resist to the limit. But seem unselfishly to consider your customers' desires, and they will naturally flock to you.

The greatest two faults in advertising lie in boasts and in selfishness. The natural instinct of a successful man is to tell what he has accomplished. He may do that to a dinner partner who cannot get away. But he cannot do that in print. Nor can he put over, at a reasonable cost, any selfish undertaking. People will listen if you talk service to them. They will turn their backs, and always, when you seek to impress an advantage for yourself. This is important. I believe that nine-tenths of the money

spent in advertising is lost because of selfish purposes blazonly presented.

The majority of advertising, even today, is based
on the plea, "Buy my brand." That plea never
appealed to anybody, and it never will. No grocer
would say, "Come to my store, not the next store."
Even in his simplicity, he is too wise for that. He
offers some advantage. Yet countless advertisers
are spending fortunes to make that attempt in print.

"Mine is the original." "Be sure to get the
genuine." All those are simply variations of the
plea, "Give me the money which you give to
others." It has no effect whatever. All of us have
too many selfish purposes to consider those of
others. A man not willing to bid for patronage
on an altruistic basis has no place in advertising
or in selling. You and I would not cede an advantage to anyone at our expense. Then don't expect that others are so different.

Permit me to use this Van Camp example as
evidence of very common shortcomings. Several
able advertising men created impressive arguments.
But not one of them knew the situation. Had they
gone from house to house, and interviewed housewives, they would have reached different conclusions. But that was too much trouble. They were
dealing with a man who knew as little as they
did about the existing conditions. Their whole
idea was to impress that man with some interesting
copy. They never got by A. D. Lasker. He was

practical. He knew that unless he sold the goods, no temporary advantage could count. So he sought out, to the best of his ability, the man who could sell the goods.

Let me pause here to emphasize the fact that favor does not count. Please the man who knows much less than you do about the consumer market, and you may get a temporary chance. But you sacrifice all that is real. In the last analysis, men are in business for profit, not to exploit their ideas. And their ideas vanish just the moment that profit fails to show.

I have never had a friend as a client. I have never had the sympathy of an advertiser in my life. Still, I respect them for their position. They desire to exploit their accomplishments, just as I do. But they represent the seller's side. I must represent the consumer. And those conceptions are usually as far apart as the poles.

Van Camp's pork and beans offered no unique arguments. They were like other pork and beans. When we met in the factory and served a half dozen brands, not a man present could decide which was Van Camp's.

But we told facts which no one else ever told. We told of beans grown on special soils. Any good navy beans must be grown there. We told of vine-ripened tomatoes, Livingston Stone tomatoes. All our competitors used them. We told how we analyzed every lot of beans, as every canner must.

We told of our steam ovens where beans are baked for hours at 245 degrees. That is regular canning practice. We told how we boiled beans in soft water to eliminate the lime which made skins tough. Our rivals did that also. We pictured the beans, whole, uncrisped, and mealy. We compared them with home-baked beans, with crisped beans on top and mushy beans below. We told why beans, when baked in home ovens, fermented and were hard to digest. And how we baked in sealed containers, so no flavor could escape.

We told just the same story that any rival could have told, but all others thought the story was too commonplace.

Then I noticed that men at their noonday luncheons downtown often ordered pork and beans. These dishes were factory-baked. Apparently these men liked factory baking better than home baking, as did I.

So we sent out men to supply Van Camp's to restaurants and lunch counters. Soon we had thousands of places serving them at noonday. We announced the fact, told the number of places, estimated how many men were every day going somewhere for Van Camp's. And that set women thinking.

Housewives were ready to quit baking beans at home. It was a long, hard task. We went after those housewives—the 94 per cent—and told them how to quit easily. We told and pictured the difference

in results. Told them how many of their men folks
were buying baked beans downtown.

There we had the arguments on our side. We
could bake better beans than any woman could
ever bake at home. But we could not bake better
beans than our rivals. So we centered our attack on
the weak spots, made Van Camp's seem the one way
out. And we created an enormous demand. Not
only that, but the Van Camp brand commanded a
much higher price than our rivals'.

Then Van Camp began producing evaporated
milk. First in one plant, later in seven or eight. He
wanted to advertise that, but we advised him
against it. Evaporated milk is a standard product.
It must be made to certain standards to meet government requirements. One cannot establish or
claim an advantage on natural or standard products. One might as well say, "Buy my eggs,
because they come from Hillside Farm." Or my butter, or my lard. Many millions of dollars have been
wasted in trying to tie people to some certain
brand of a staple; to brands of flour or oatmeal,
and to many staple products like those. About all
one can say is: "Buy my brand. Give me the money
that you give to others. Insist that I get it." Those
are not popular appeals.

I analyzed the situation on evaporated milk. I
found that certain brands, regardless of advertising, dominated and controlled certain markets.
Some they had held for many years against all

efforts to displace them. The only reason seemed to be a familiar brand. Housewives naturally continue on the brands they know.

So I devised a plan for making Van Camp's Milk familiar. In a page ad. I inserted a coupon, good at any store for a ten-cent can. We paid the grocer his retail price. For three weeks we announced that this ad. would appear. At the same time we told the story of Van Camp's Evaporated Milk.

We sent copies of these ads. to all grocers, and told them that every customer of theirs would receive one of these coupons. It was evident that they must have Van Camp's Milk. Every coupon meant a ten-cent sale which, if they missed it, would go to a competitor.

The result was almost universal distribution, and at once.

We proved out this plan in several cities of moderate size. Then we undertook New York City. There the market was dominated by a rival brand. Van Camp had slight distribution. In three weeks we secured, largely by letter, 97 per cent distribution. Every grocer saw the necessity of being prepared for that coupon demand.

In the meantime we announced in the newspapers the coupon that was to appear. We told housewives what to expect in this milk. And we tried to convert them from bottled milk to evaporated.

Then one Sunday in a page ad. we inserted the coupon. This just in Greater New York. As a result of that ad. 1,460,000 coupons were presented. We paid $146,000 to the grocers to redeem them. But 1,460,000 homes were trying Van Camp's Milk after reading our story, and all in a single day.

The total cost of that enterprise, including the advertising, was $175,000, mostly spent in redeeming those coupons. In less than nine months that cost came back with a profit. We captured the New York market. And Van Camp has held it ever since with enormous yearly sales.

Compare that method with distributing samples from house to house. There you are offering something unasked-for and unwanted. It has no prestige. The very giving of a sample cheapens the product, when done in that careless way. The stores are not stocked. Grocers are offended by your free distribution of things they sell.

Under our plan, grocers had to stock. The woman to get a sample had to make an effort. She could not know of the sample without reading the facts about this milk. If she presented the coupon, it was because the ads. had led her to desire this product. The grocer made his profit on the sale, so he was happy. The woman found Van Camp's in stock when she used that sample can. Thus we captured market after market, and we held them. No casual sample distributor ever made an impression on them. Such is the difference between making a show and really getting what you are after.

Few makers of evaporated milk can accomplish national distribution. They cannot produce enough milk. So the problem there usually is to develop local markets to take care of increased production.

The time came when rivals used our sample plan and we had to invent something else. Millions of homes had by that time been converted to evaporated milk. The sale had reached 24,000,000 cases annually. The main question then was to establish a familiar brand.

Then in new cities which we tried to capture we offered a secret gift. We offered to mail the housewife a present if she sent us the labels from six Van Camp cans. Or we piled wrapped presents in the grocers' store windows, without telling what they were. Any woman could get one by buying six cans of Van Camp's.

Curiosity is a strong factor in human nature, and especially with women. Describe a gift, and some will decide that they want it, more will decide that they don't. But everybody wants a secret gift.

There are things to consider in such an offer. The gift must not be disappointing. It should be somewhat better than women are led to expect. Then the offer must be treated in a rather insiduous way.

The result of this offer was to induce countless women to buy six cans of Van Camp's Milk. They paid regular price, but they received a gift which made the bargain attractive. The gift cost more than our profits on the sale. But milk is in daily consumption. There is hardly a limit to what one can pay to get a new user established. The six cans made Van Camp's a familiar brand. The user had read all about Van Camp's. She was ready to find it superior. So she asked for Van Camp's when she needed a new supply. We captured and held many a big market in that way.

The reader may say this is sampling, it is scheming and merchandising, not dignified advertising as we know it. I have no sympathy with dignified and orthodox advertising. We are in business to get results. The finest palaver in the world, if it fails to pay, is useless. Hundreds of millions of dollars, every year, are being wasted on it.

I want to sell what I have to sell, and sell it at a profit. I want the figures on cost and result. We can pose as artists and as geniuses for only a little while. Business men find us out. Those who have tried that plan have perished—every one I know. But a real result-getter never loses his charm.

We meet men sometimes whose ideas are centered on the non-essentials. They want to boast of their accomplishments. And they are often big men in some ways. One can easily please them if he wishes to sacrifice all practical ideas, for advertising to them is a maze. But do that and you are bound to lose. The ultimate object of business is profit. Cater to any other side, and you will shortly find yourself discredited.

I have lost many an account because I refused to feature an institution. Or to foster some personal pride. But I have always found that the seekers for profit were in the vast majority. Men are crying for new ways to make money. Discover those ways, find out how to promote them, and you will have offered ten times the work one man can ever do. Not literary work, not work which leads your lady friends to say, "That's wonderful." But practical selling. No man save a dilettante will ever try for anything else.

Chapter Ten

Automobile
advertising

I wrote my first advertisements on automobiles
in 1899. They referred to a steam car made in
Milwaukee. My book on the car was entitled *The
Sport of Kings*. The model I owned was the first
motor car in Racine. My first day of ownership
cost me $300, through the scaring of hack horses
and other forms of damage.

I was chauffeur and garage man. It required
thirty minutes to start the car, which we had to
count on in catching a train. And on more than
that. Starting was a small problem when compared
with keeping the car going. When we drove ten
miles without a breakdown we boasted of the record. When we ever got through to Milwaukee—
about twenty-five miles—we went directly to the
factory for repairs, and we rarely returned that
day.

Every ten miles we stopped for water. Then we watched the boiler gauge. As the car moved it pumped water, but it often moved too slowly on the roads of those days to keep the boiler supplied. Our seat was on top of the boiler. I remember nights on muddy roads when we watched the water gauge go down. At a certain point we knew the boiler would explode, but we kept on going to shorten our walk back home. There are pleasanter experiences than sitting on a boiler on a gloomy night waiting for it to explode, and contemplating the long muddy road ahead.

But that experience made me an automobile enthusiast. In the time since then I have written successful automobile ads. about some twenty cars.

In my early days with Lord & Thomas, Hugh Chalmers bought out the Thomas-Detroit car, and he came to consult me about it. Mr. Chalmers was a remarkable man. He had been, it was said, the highest-paid sales manager in the United States, with the National Cash Register Company. I learned much of salesmanship from him. And I was gratified to note that in all our years together he and I never disagreed.

The problems in automobile advertising then were different from the problems now. For years the situation was constantly changing, like a kaleidoscope. One had to keep well informed to strike the responsive chord.

I featured Howard E. Coffin, then chief engineer for the Chalmers Company. You will note that wherever possible I inject some personality into an advertising campaign. This has always proved itself an impressive idea. People like to deal with men whose names are connected with certain accomplishments. They would rather do that, I have found, than deal with soulless corporations. Naming an expert in an advertising campaign indicates a man of unique ability and prominence. He may be unknown to the public. He generally is at the start. But when a manufacturer features him, people accord him respect. He soon becomes famous, then his name becomes an exclusive feature of great value. Howard Coffin was unknown when I first featured him. Advertising gave him such prominence that he was made head of the Aircraft Board in the war.

For somewhat similar reasons, an individual's name is usually better than a coined name on a product. And far better than a trade mark. It locates the sponsor as a man proud of his creation. It is far easier to make a man famous than an institution. Consider how much names count in theatrical productions, in the movies, or in authorship. They are often names created for the purpose. It is also so in merchandising.

In those early days Cadillac and Chalmers cars sold at about the same price—around $1,500. Cadillac had an older reputation and it was a much handsomer car. But the featuring of Howard E. Coffin gave to the Chalmers a distinction which brought it great success.

We met other conditions as they came up. We found a growing impression that automobile profits were excessive. We met the situation with headlines announcing, "Our Profit is 9 Per Cent." Then we stated the actual costs on many hidden parts. The total was over $700, and it omitted all the conspicuous parts, like the body, upholstery, etc.

That brings up another point in advertising— the advantage of being specific. Platitudes and generalities make no more impression than water on a duck. To say, "Best in the world," "Cheapest in the long run," "The most economical," etc., does not create conviction. Such claims are expected. The most carefully censored magazines accept them as merely expressions of a salesman trying to put his best foot forward. They are not classed as falsehoods, but as mere exaggerations. They probably do more harm than good, because they indicate a looseness of expression and cause people to discount whatever you say.

But when we make specific and definite claims, when we state actual figures or facts, we indicate weighed and measured expressions. We are telling either the truth or a lie. People do not expect big concerns to lie. They know that we cannot lie in the best mediums. So we get full credit for those claims. I shall have other occasions to cite the advantages of definite, specific claims.

The Hudson Company was an offshoot of the Chalmers Company. Mr. Chalmers was interested. The Hudson Company was organized because the Chalmers Company was over-manned in the selling end. Howard E. Coffin went with the Hudson, and I featured him there. But we went further. We pictured and named our board of forty-eight engineers. Thus we advertised the Hudson as an engineering accomplishment. That accorded with the conditions of the times. Motor cars were not then perfected. Troubles were common. The average buyer thought more of good engineering than of any other factor. We made the Hudson stand for that in a very conspicuous way.

That proved itself a sound foundation. The Hudson car has been a great success, and it remains so still. The reason lies largely in that underpinning which we built in those early days. I advertised the Hudson car for seven years, then relinquished the advertising to a protégé of mine who continued very similar policies.

The story of the Overland reads like a romance. Mr. John Willys ran a store in Elmira, N. Y., called the Elmira Arms Co. He sold bicycles. Then, when the automobile made its appearance, he secured the agency for the Overland, then built at Indianapolis.

The Overland proved itself at that time one of the few satisfactory cars. One sold another, until the demand in the Elmira territory far exceeded the supply. Mr. Willys took orders with deposits, and sent the deposits down to Indianapolis. But the cars failed to come. So he went to Indianapolis to learn the reason, and arrived on a Sunday morning. He met the Overland owners at the hotel, and they told him they were bankrupt. They had failed to meet their payroll the night before. They owed some $45,000 more than they could pay. Mr. Willys could not return his deposits, so he sought for a way to obtain the cars.

He said: "If you are bankrupt you cannot continue the business."

"No," they replied, "we are quitting."

"Then suppose I can continue it," Mr. Willys said. "Will you turn it over to me, debts and all?"

They told him they would. The defaulted payroll was $450. Mr. Willys set about to raise it. He borrowed some money from the hotel clerk. He had a little of his own. The next morning he called the workmen together and paid them the wages due. Then he said: "Get together a car. Find parts enough, and quickly. We must raise more money."

They did put together a car, and Mr. Willys shipped it to a friend in Allentown, Pa. With it he sent a letter somewhat as follows: "Dear Albert: I have shipped you an Overland car, sight draft with bill lading attached. It is necessary that you accept it, for I have cashed the sight draft and have used the money."

"Dear Albert" did accept it. Then they made up other cars and shipped them in the same way. About four in five of them stuck. The demand came for more cars, and the problem of financing became acute.

Mr. Willys went to the creditors with his famous inimitable smile. He said: "You will get nothing if you close us up, for we have nothing there. But give me a chance and I will try to pull through and pay you every dollar we owe." The creditors accepted that proposition, because they saw no other way out.

Mr. Willys raised some more money—a very little—and went on. Soon the factory capacity was oversold. There was no time to build more plants, so he erected tents. And in those tents he made that season, I believe, $365,000.

I do not vouch for all the figures. I am telling the story from memory. But the essentials are correct and indicative.

Then Mr. Willys decided to go back to Elmira and build a factory there. That was his home town. While he was shaving one night to take the train, his agent in Toledo called him up. He told of a plant in Toledo—the Pope-Toledo plant—which was closed and bankrupt. He said: "Come and see it. You will find it wonderfully equipped. And you will find steel enough and parts enough to pay the price they ask."

As a result, Mr. Willys stopped off at Toledo. He walked through the plant the next day, then went on to New York and bought it. The next day he sailed for Europe. When he returned he found that his people had sold the steel alone for far more than the cost of the plant.

As I said before, this story may not be quite accurate, but it illustrates the point I bring out. The essentials are there.

The next season I took up the Overland advertising—the first advertising they ever did. I analyzed the situation to find its most appealing features. But nothing in all the data I gathered appealed to me like the romance. So my first ads. were headed "The Wonderful Overland Story." I told how demands from users had led John E. Willys to undertake to supply them. How that demand had grown and grown, until it was necessary to erect a plant of tents.

Again that limelights a principle in advertising. People are like sheep. They cannot judge values, nor can you and I. We judge things largely by others' impressions, by popular favor. We go with the crowd. So the most effective thing I have ever found in advertising is the trend of the crowd.

That is a factor not to be overlooked. People follow styles and preferences. We rarely decide for ourselves, because we don't know the facts. But when we see the crowds taking any certain direction, we are much inclined to go with them.

I showed in my advertising how the crowds were going to Overland automobiles. I told how the demand had forced a bankrupt concern into solvency. Then how it created a tent city. That presentation set people thinking. And they followed the trend. The Overland became, as it is today, one of the largest-selling cars in the world.

The Reo at one time had a bad season. The season's output was unsold and sales had practically stopped. The next season's outlook was dubious. I was called in to meet this emergency. That has been my chief work in advertising—meeting emergencies. Nobody ever called me in when the skies were bright and the seas were calm. Nearly every client quit me when he got into smooth waters.

That was partly my fault, for I liked emergencies. I would rather be a pilot than a captain. When an advertising ship got on its clear course, I lost much interest in it. The work became monotonous. I was always ready to drop off and pilot another.

Then continuous advertising along one line grows monotonous to the advertiser. He feels that the public reads his story as often as does he. So in the course of time he comes to desire a change.

I could never agree with this viewpoint. When I find what seems to be the right course I always wish to keep it. There may be another way to success, even to greater success. But the chances are against it. The ways to great success in any line are not numerous. When a certain method has proved itself profitable I hesitate to drop it, until I have found and proved a better method by some local tests. The best way found to sell a product to thousands is probably the best way to sell other thousands.

Every ad., in my opinion, should tell a complete story. It should include every fact and argument found to be valuable. Most people, I figure, read a story but once, as they do a news item. I know of no reason why they should read it again. So I wish them to get in that one reading every convincing fact.

Any complete story told over and over is bound to grow monotonous to the man who reads all ads. It bores the man who writes it. Both the writer and reader come to long for a change.

I studied the Reo situation, then went away to consider it. The car was built by Mr. R. E. Olds, one of the original motor-car builders. I considered that fact, the existing misfortunes, and all competition that affected the case. The difficult conditions called for effective measures.

In a few days I went back and told Mr. Olds that I would undertake the advertising on three conditions. The first was that he name the new model Reo the Fifth. That to give a distinctive name and to emphasize the fact that we had a new model.

The next condition was that Mr. Olds sign the ads. That to gain full effect from his great reputation. I told him I would write ads. he would be proud to sign, and he agreed.

Then I stipulated that he call it "My Farewell Car." That to signify a degree of finality and his satisfaction with it. "But," he replied, "I don't intend to retire." I said that was unnecessary. Sarah Bernhardt made seven farewell tours. He could have two or three. Every farewell is subject to reconsideration.

So we came out with ads. headed "My Farewell Car" and signed "R. E. Olds, Designer." The ads. were written to typify the man, the man of rugged honesty, of vast experience. The man who knew. The man who scorned to do anything but the best that was possible, regardless of its cost. The man who put his reputation far ahead of profit.

The campaign from the start was a sensational success. Reo the Fifth became at once the most conspicuous car of the year. A new era dawned for the Reo Company, and that era has continued until that concern is one of the soundest and most successful in the field.

The most successful automobile advertising I ever did resulted in disaster, due to other causes. That was the Mitchell advertising. I was called there to meet an emergency. As always, I gave an enormous amount of study to the automobile situation, to current ideas and trends. I concluded that the best key-note was efficiency. Efficiency was then a popular subject with men in all lines of business.

The Mitchell Company had an able efficiency

expert. They had a very efficient plant. So I came out with ads. headed, "John W. Bate, Efficiency Expert," and I told of the man and his methods.

That campaign was also a sensation. I never knew any automobile advertising to bring so many inquiries. Sales started at an amazing rate. I had struck the popular chord. Buyers of motor cars wanted, above all else, economies due to efficiency. Soon the company was on the road to great success. It was recapitalized in a large way. But the car was a fizzle. Its engineers had skimped in every detail. Hundreds of cars came back, and every car sold blighted the name Mitchell. The larger the sales the worse became the ruin. The very success of the advertising, with the car that was offered, led to destruction. We played too high a note for the product we had to sell. The bad reputation was so widely spread that recovery proved impossible. That formed another lesson in advertising.

In 1924 I was called on to advertise the Studebaker car. For several years I had been out of the automobile field. I had to educate myself in existing conditions. That is always essential. One can never strike the right chord until he knows the trend of popular opinion.

I studied the situation for weeks. Studebaker had been a tremendous success. The multiplying sales, increasing assets and profits, had become a stock-market sensation. I concluded that those facts, always encouraging to men watching the weather, had been a major factor in Studebaker success. So I decided to build upon them.

The result was a campaign with which all are familiar. We cited those multiplying sales. We stated the assets and the facilities they embodied. We showed by actual figures how quantity production reduced costs. We told the cost of certain features compared with features used by others. We gave actual figures, and we showed how we could afford those extravagances by producing 150,000 cars per year. That proved a new note, and today an ultimate note, in automobile advertising.

The lesson in this is the lesson in all salesmanship. One must know what buyers are thinking about and what they are coming to want. One must know the trends to be a leader in a winning trend.

Advertising to many is mere ad.-writing. Language and style are considered important. They are not. If fine writing is effective in any way it is a detriment. It suggests an effort to sell. And every effort to sell creates corresponding resistance.

Salesmanship-in-print is exactly the same as salesmanship-in-person. Style is a handicap. Anything that takes attention from the subject reduces the impression. One may say: "That is a beautiful ad. The pictures are perfect, the presentation is wonderful." But that very idea prohibits one from being influenced by the ad. It indicates lack of sincerity. It suggests an effort to sell. And we are all on our guard when somebody, apparently, is trying to get our money away.

The only way to sell is in some way to seem to offer super-service. It may be offered in a crude way. The majority of advertising successes have been accomplished in crude ways. They struck a human chord in a human way. They seemed to offer wanted service. That is why so much "fine advertising" fails to bring results. People are wary of it. And why so many successes are made in ways that seem crude. They are made by super-salesmen who forget themselves.

Chapter Eleven

Tire
advertising

I t was also my lot to pioneer tire advertising. Tires had been advertised somewhat since bicycle days, but with scarcely more than a name. The Goodyear Company had for many years been customers of our agency. I believe that their expenditure never exceeded $40,000 per year. Nobody suspected that tires could be popularized.

One day it occurred to us that we could increase our advertising business by increasing accounts on our books. Thereafter that became our dominant principle. Along those lines we grew to be one of the largest agencies in the world.

Commissions to advertising agents are paid by the publishers. Not for changing accounts from one agency to another, but for increasing the volume of advertising. We should earn our pay. One way is by seeking and developing new advertising opportunities. Another is by making it possible for existing advertisers to multiply expenditures.

I have rarely taken an account from another advertising agent. I have never tried to do so, save where a big opportunity was being spoiled by wrong methods. Nearly all my large accounts have been of my own creation. I have started with small sums sometimes, and made the advertising grow out of earnings. Such developments form the real satisfactions of advertising.

The Goodyear people, after much persuasion, were induced to enlarge their expenditure. For the first season they gave us $200,000. It seemed to them a reckless amount.

They were then pioneering what they called the straight-side tire. I had heard about it, but did not know what it was. Ads. about it had frequently come to my desk. I was interested both in tires and in advertising, but was never enough impressed to learn what straight-side meant.

I asked them about it and they showed me the difference between straight-side and clincher tires. I asked the reason for that difference. They told me the straight-side would not rim-cut. And that type of construction had, size for size, 10 per cent greater air capacity.

"Then why," I asked, "don't you emphasize those results? Results are what men are after. They care not how you get them."

That was a new idea to them. They were manufacturers, interested mainly in a type of construction. Being interested in manufacturing details, they naturally talked them to the public.

There lies the chief reason why no manufacturer should ever conduct his own advertising. Few attempt it now. The advertiser is too close to his factory. His own interests tend to blind him to the interests of his customers. He fails to appreciate the consumer's side.

He tells of the things he takes pride in—his methods and processes, the size of his plant, the age of his business, etc. The advertising man must study the consumer and tell what he wants to know.

I coined the name "No-Rim-Cut Tires." Across every ad. we ran the heading, "No-Rim-Cut Tires, 10% Oversize." The results were immediate and enormous. Sales grew by leaps and bounds. Goodyear tires soon occupied the leading place in tiredom.

Another result was to force all rivals to this type of tire. In two or three years the time came when Goodyear, on that point, could not claim advantage. So we gradually reduced the name No-Rim-Cut and featured the name Goodyear.

By that time, however, we had another talking point even more impressive. That was the sensational growth in demand. We featured it in pictures and in type, until it seemed that the whole motor world was turning to Goodyear tires.

That is in most lines a great selling argument. People follow the crowds. It is hard for them in most things to analyze reasons and worth, so they accept the verdict of the majority.

We did another thing there through a name. We called the anti-skid-tread All-Weather. We figured out what claim could count most and made the name imply it. So the name told our main story. It formed an ad. in itself. Our main purpose then was to induce motorists to use this type of tire on all wheels in all weathers. That has since become the custom, largely through that influence.

There is a great advantage in a name that tells a story. The name is usually displayed. Thus the right name may form a reasonably complete ad. which all who run may read. Coining the right name is often the major step in good advertising. No doubt such names often double the results of expenditures. Consider the value of such names as May-Breath, Dyanshine, 3-in-One Oil, Palmolive Soap, etc.

Another problem we had to solve was to get dealers to carry tire stocks. Few of them did so in those days. They bought from the Goodyear branches as they sold. We prepared a large newspaper campaign and offered to name in each ad. all the dealers who stocked. The minimum requirement was a $250 stock. In a few months we induced some 30,000 dealers to stock Goodyear tires on that basis. And that campaign did much to change the whole complexion of the tire business.

This naming of dealers in local advertising is an almost irresistible inducement to stock. Few plans are more effective. No dealer likes to see his rivals named in a big campaign and his own name omitted. The more who join in the plan the easier it is to get others. I have often secured on new products almost universal distribution in this way.

The Goodyear campaign was one of my greatest successes. It placed Goodyear tires in the lead. Never have I met changing situations in more effective ways. The advertising grew from $40,000 to nearly $2,000,000 per year.

Still I lost it. There developed a desire for institutional advertising which I never could approve. It is natural. Great success brings to most men a desire to boast a little. But boasting is the last thing people want to hear. Men like to picture their plants, to tell how they grew, and to preach a little on methods and policies. That may be satisfying, but it isn't salesmanship. No man in advertising, or in anything else, can afford to offend his own principles. The moment he compromises for money's sake he is lost. Not as a success, perhaps, but as an artist. As a man who contributes to his profession or calling and brings it to higher levels.

There lies the cause of most conflicts in advertising. The layman pays the bills. He naturally assumes the right to dictate. He is not apt to exercise that right in the early stages. The scheme is too new to him. But there comes a time when he feels that he is also an advertising expert. It is curious how we all desire to excel in something outside of our province.

That leads many men astray. Men make money in one business and lose it in many others. They seem to feel that one success makes them super-business men.

These men would not venture to dictate to a surgeon. Or tell a lawyer how to win a certain case. Or an artist how to paint a picture. They recognize technical knowledge in vocations like those. But not in advertising, which seems so simple to them, because it aims at simple people. They do not realize that no lifetime is long enough to learn much more than the rudiments.

Later I advertised Miller tires. The situation had changed entirely. Buyers in general had come to regard good tires as about alike. It was necessary to upset that impression and to secure a preference in some way.

Miller tires were largely used on bus lines on the Pacific coast. I secured the data and the records. The figures on buses using Miller tires were impressive. The mileage records were surprising. The trend toward Millers in commercial uses was significant.

I made those facts the key-note of my campaign.

The ordinary tire buyer makes no comparisons. He rarely keeps track of tire mileage. When he does so, it is not done in a scientific way. But he knows that large tire users do not adopt a certain make on guess. I played on that knowledge. I stated in exact figures the results of comparisons. I pictured the trend toward Millers in commercial uses where men knew to exactness what they were doing.

I told of the tests made in the Miller factory, where great machines wore out all sorts of tires under actual road conditions. How tires were studied which showed the least advantage over Millers. I created the impression—and a right impression—that the Miller people were doing their utmost to secure the maximum tire mileage. That was a short but successful campaign.

Our difference there, as in many lines, lay between dealers and consumers. My idea is that we cannot afford to sell anything twice. We cannot spend large sums in expense and concessions in selling our goods to dealers. Then spend other large sums in selling for the dealer. The tax is too great on the consumer. We must choose.

If a line can be sold by interesting dealers, let the dealer sell. But if we are going to sell our goods for him, we cannot pay him more than the profit of a mere distributor.

The greatest calamities in advertising come through doubling the selling expense. The advertiser wins the consumer, and that is expense enough. Then he gives his profits to jobbers and dealers in an effort to interest them. He gives free goods and other costly inducements, and gets nothing at all. The dealers and jobbers supply the demand. They become mere order-takers.

There is one of the greatest questions in merchandising. An unadvertised line without consumer demand must depend on distributors. And they demand a big toll. But however large you make it, somebody else will bid higher. The margin soon diminishes to insignificance.

If you are an advertiser, creating consumer demand, you must ignore to some extent these intermediary factors. Treat them fairly, but do not pay them for what they cannot do. The jobber will charge you, if you let him, his expense of competition. The dealer will compare your allotted profits with profits on lines he owns. They do not figure that in one case you do the selling; in the other they do it all.

Most lines which I have advertised have never employed a salesman. The whole idea has been to win consumers and let them sell to dealers and to jobbers. Those who have tried to sell to consumers, then to dealers and jobbers, have attained prohibitive expense. One must choose. Margins in selling are not sufficient to accommodate both factors.

Chapter Twelve

Early history
of Palmolive

We organized in our agency an "advisory board" over which I presided. We announced that anyone could bring there advertising problems, in person or by letter, and receive without obligation the advice of the best men in our agency. Some sixteen able advertising men sat around the table. They offered an inviting opportunity to advertisers, existing or prospective. Some hundreds of men with dubious prospects came there and we advised nineteen in twenty of them not to proceed. The men who hesitated were large advertisers who had most at stake. That is generally so in this line.

Our object in these meetings was to foster good advertising, to warn men against mistakes, and to try to discover in the mass of suggestions some jewels of advertising opportunities. Under the same policy we published numerous books offering advice based on our many experiences. We felt that our own interests depended on the prosperity of advertising as a whole. Mistakes and disasters hurt advertising. One conspicuous success may encourage many ventures. No doubt our helpful and unselfish policy was a large factor in the growth of advertising during the past twenty years.

One morning there appeared at our meeting Mr. B. J. Johnson of the B. J. Johnson Soap Co. of Milwaukee. With him came Mr. Charles Pearce, a newly-appointed sales manager who was seeking a way to make good. They came to discuss Galvanic Soap—a laundry soap. After due consideration we advised them against entering that advertising field. It is too difficult, too hard fought to offer encouragement to a new advertiser. On the facts we cited the owners soon came to agree with us.

Then we asked if they had anything else. They said that they had a toilet soap called Palmolive, made with palm and olive oils. It had slight distribution; they had not considered it as an advertising possibility.

At that time the men around the table only dimly recognized the strength of the beauty appeal. We were destined to later develop on that line some of the greatest advertising successes. There is no stronger appeal to women. One man suggested that Cleopatra used palm and olive oils. Another reminded us that Roman beauties did

likewise. Gradually we came to recognize the germ
of an advertising opportunity, and we asked the
soap-makers to let us make an experiment. We suggested a trial in Grand Rapids, Michigan, and we
estimated that it could be made for about $1,000.
But that was too much money to stake on so uncertain a venture, so we were forced to compromise on Benton Harbor, Michigan, where the cost
was $700. In that little city appeared the first ads.
on Palmolive Soap.

We evolved a plan of introduction which I have
used in many of my best campaigns. I originated
that plan, so far as I know, and it has been one of
the chief factors in my success. We ran two or
three ads. telling the story of Palmolive Soap,
bringing out the beauty appeal. Above the ads. in
a box we announced that in a few days we would
buy a cake of Palmolive for every woman who
applied. That offer multiplied the readers of our
ads. When you offer to buy something for a woman,
she wants to learn about it. Thus we interested
most women readers in our complexion soap. When
we felt that we had created a sufficient desire
for it we came out with a page ad. with a coupon
good at any store for a ten-cent cake. The coupon
authorized the dealer to deliver one cake to the
bearer and charge us ten cents for it.

This plan has many advantages over a "free"
offer. It is much more impressive, for one thing.
There is considerable difference in the psychologi-

cal effect when you offer to buy an article for a woman to try, and pay the dealer his price for it, as compared with offering that article free to all. The "free" offer cheapens a product. There is a certain resistance when we ask people to afterward pay for a product which came to them first as a gift. But when we ourselves buy the article, just as the consumer does, we show supreme confidence in the belief that the article will please. "We Will Buy" is a much better headline than "10-Cent Cake Free."

Then the buying method forces dealers to stock the product you offer. No salesmen are needed. Simply mail a proof of the coupon ad. to dealers. Point out the fact that practically every home will receive it. Also that the coupon is as good as a dime. Women will not throw it away. If one dealer fails to redeem it another dealer will. We gain by this plan universal distribution immediately at moderate cost. That is, of course, the first essential in advertising.

Run in any community a few ads. announcing a buying offer and you are sure of a pretty general reading of your proposition. Then when the page ad. appears with the coupon, all who are interested in your product will present it. Thus we gain in two weeks a general understanding of our product and users by the thousands.

I have never found that it paid to give either a sample or a full-size package to people who do not request it. We must arouse interest in our product before it has value to anybody. I consider promiscuous sampling a very bad plan indeed. Products handed out without asking or thrown on the doorstep lose respect. It is different when you force people to make an effort or when you buy the product at retail price on request.

Such was the plan we used in Benton Harbor on the initial Palmolive ads. The cost, including the redemption of coupons, was $700, I believe. As a result several thousand women were started on this soap with full knowledge of its qualities and purpose. Then we waited to see the effect. What would users do when they tried the soap? The answer to that question is the most vital factor in advertising.

Now I come to some figures which may not be exact. This campaign was started in 1911. My memory may be somewhat, but not seriously, at fault. The repeat sales in Benton Harbor paid for the advertising before the bills were due. We knew then we had struck a responsive chord. We knew we had a winner.

We tried the same test ads. in numerous other cities, always with like results. I believe that they spent about $50,000 in local advertising to prove that our appeal was effective. Always the advertising paid for itself as we went along. Then we went into magazines and gained national distribution and sale in ways I shall describe.

Let me pause for a few remarks. In the tales I recite in this history there is no desire to over-emphasize any parts I played. Our agency was an organization of experienced men who worked together. The head of the agency often said that we never succeeded for any body who could not have succeeded without us. I do not agree with him. On most of our successes we were the ones to discover and develop the advertising opportunities. That was naturally so because that was our business. The plan, the theory, and the strategy of the advertising all were our creations. But one necessity was an acceptable product. That depended on the makers. Another necessity was good business management. I consider the Palmolive success as particularly due to that after the route was discovered. The leading factor was the Charles Pearce who came to us that fateful morning in 1911.

The purpose of this business biography is not to claim personal credit. It is to point out to those who follow me certain principles which I discovered by hard work. I have no wish to minimize any other person's part or hurt anybody's pride. No business is created by one man.

After those local newspaper tests on Palmolive it was decided to attain national distribution quickly. There we followed the same lines as in our local efforts. We contracted for a page in the *Saturday Evening Post* and *Ladies' Home Journal.*

There we inserted a coupon good at any drug store in the country for a ten-cent cake of Palmolive. We sent advance proofs of that page to druggists everywhere, giving figures on the circulation by localities, and pointing out that the coupon was as good as a dime to the woman and the druggist. As a result we received orders from everywhere for a soap which the dealers had never seen. As I remember, those advance orders exceeded $100,000.

Jobbers were well stocked—on consignment, I think—so that dealers could quickly get new supplies. When the ads came out the coupon demand was tremendous. After a few days tens of thousands of women were using Palmolive Soap, seeking the virtues described in our advertising. And the drug stores of the country, almost to a store, were supplying it. The results in repeat sales were even better than in our local appeals.

Such were the ways in which Palmolive Soap was established, so far as advertising was concerned. Now the sales run to many millions yearly. Palmolive is the leading toilet soap of the world. The annual advertising expenditure runs into enormous figures. Makers, advertising agents, and publishers have gained fortunes in the evolution of this $700 test.

Some lessons I would like to draw are these: Human nature our country over is about alike. The appeal which won in Benton Harbor won from coast to coast.

One does not need to sell a product twice. One can rarely afford to sell to both dealers and consumers. If you sell the consumer the dealer will supply the demand. That is more important today than in old days. Both personal salesmanship and advertising are more costly than they were.

Quick volume is more profitable than slowly-developed volume. When one proves that a plan is right and safe the great object is quick development. Attain the maximum as soon as you can.

The simple things, easily understood, striking a popular chord, are the appeals which succeed with the masses. They often sound to the intellectual like excerpts from Mother Goose. Dutch Cleanser chases dirt, Ivory Soap floats, Gold Dust Twins do your work, Children Cry for Castoria, Keep Your Schoolgirl Complexion—such things win the nine-tenths.

I once knew a man who was advertising business books. They were instructive, based on exceptional experience, books that any business man should read. But the publisher could not sell them at a profit. He consulted an advertising expert in our office. About all the expert did was to suggest the announcement, "Your name will be printed in gilt on each book." We might naturally say that such an announcement to a business man would not prove important. But it made that set of books a success. It gave the books some distinction, some personality that won, beyond all the logical arguments.

A life insurance company solicits business by mail from men considered wise. The usual arguments would stir few men to action. But this company states that a leather-covered memorandum book with his name in gilt is waiting for his acceptance. Simply tell them where to send it. At the same time tell them the date of your birth, etc.—facts on which to present an insurance proposition.

This offer, I believe, goes only to men of affairs. Men who are supposed to be absorbed in large business problems. But it gains a reply from a very large percentage. Those men of affairs dislike to think that some little book which belongs to them —perhaps a ten-cent book—is being overlooked. Such is human nature.

Now back to the Palmolive Company. The success of Palmolive Soap led these good people into many advertising adventures. Most of them were fizzles, as with the majority of such undertakings. Neither they nor we had the magic to do the impossible things.

One was Palmolive Shampoo. They had on that no unique claims. It was simply a good shampoo. The appeal presented was, "Buy my brand instead of the other fellow's" and such appeals never go far.

In an island near Japan there grows an oil famous for growing hair. I have before me photographs of Japanese women standing on chairs with their hair floating on the floor. The whole supply of the oil had been contracted for years by French hair-tonic makers. The contracts had expired. I urged the Palmolive people to secure that oil and argument, but the cost was high.

I do not know what has been done on Palmolive Shampoo by merchandising methods. But I have had much experience with other shampoos. And I know that nobody in a hard-fought field has ever succeeded without some exceptional claims.

On the other side let me recite the experience with Palmolive Shaving Cream. That was a logical adaptation of the fame of Palmolive Soap. But certain facts had to be considered. Practically all the users of shaving cream were wedded to certain brands. Perhaps most of them had used those brands for years, and they liked them. Our problem was to win users from one brand to another.

One can hardly claim in a shaving soap exceptional effects. That is not logical. Some of the greatest soap-makers in the country have studied shaving soaps for years. But they have never stated in exact terms their accomplishments.

I sent out some research men to interview men by the hundreds. I asked them what they most desired in a shaving cream. Then I took those answers to Milwaukee, then the home of Palmolive, and submitted them to V. C. Cassidy, chief chemist. I said: "These are the factors men want. They may get them in other shaving creams, but nobody yet has told them. Give me actual data on these results as applied to Palmolive Shaving Cream."

Men wanted abundant lather. Cassidy proved that Palmolive Shaving Cream multiplied itself in lather 250 times. Men wanted quick action. The Palmolive chemists proved by tests that within one minute the beard absorbed 15 per cent of water, and that made the hairs wax-like for cutting.

Men wanted enduring lather. Chemists proved that Palmolive Shaving Cream maintained its creamy fulness for ten minutes on the face.

Palm and olive oils were accepted as a lotion. But I asked Mr. Cassidy if there was anything else which the ordinary man did not realize on shaving cream. He said that the greatest factor was unrecognized. The reason why men could not use in shaving an ordinary toilet soap. That is the fact that the bubbles are not strong and enduring. They must wedge in between the hairs and hold them erect, like wheat prepared for mowing. So we claimed for Palmolive Shaving Cream, and rightly, bubbles that meet the requirements.

Probably other shaving creams could meet the same specifications. I have no idea that one man far excels some others in this line. But we were the first to give figures on results. And one actual figure counts for more than countless platitudes.

I am told that in eighteen months Palmolive Shaving Cream dominated the field it entered. If so, it was because we substituted actual figures for atmospheric claims.

Anybody who reads this, interested in real advertising, should get the points I introduce. You cannot go into a well-occupied field on the simple appeal, "buy my brand." That is a selfish appeal, repugnant to all. One must offer exceptional service to induce people to change from favorite brands to yours. The usual advertiser does not offer that exceptional service. It cannot be expected. But giving exact figures on that service which others fail to supply may establish great advantage.

Take the example of Mazda lamps, or tungsten lamps in general. The claim that they give more light than carbon lamps makes slight impression. Everybody expects one seller to claim advantage over others. But when you state that tungsten lamps multiply efficiency three times over, that is something for all to consider.

Back of all of which lies the principle of personal salesmanship. All advertising should be based on that. Meeting a woman at her door is much like meeting her around her evening lamp. The same principles of salesmanship apply. And advertising is salesmanship-in-print.

Chapter Thirteen

Puffed grains
and Quaker Oats

O ne of my greatest successes came about
through advertising Puffed Wheat and Puffed
Rice. And it came about in this way.

Mr. H. P. Crowell, the president of The Quaker
Oats Company, was a friend of an old associate of
mine. That associate urged Mr. Crowell to learn
what I could do to help him. So one day Mr. Crowell called me to his office and said something like
this: "We have our long-established advertising
connections, and they are satisfactory. But we have
many lines not advertised. If you can find one which
offers opportunity, we will experiment with you.
We will spend $50,000 or over to prove out your
ideas."

I looked over the line, and I found two appealing products. One was called Puffed Rice; the other
was called Wheat Berries. The Rice was selling at

10 cents then, and the Wheat was advertised at 7 cents. The sales had been declining. The makers were convinced that the products could not succeed.

I selected those products because of their unique appeals. I urged them to change the name of Wheat Berries to Puffed Wheat, so we could advertise the two puffed grains together. I asked them to change prices, so that Puffed Rice sold at 15 cents and Puffed Wheat at 10 cents. This added an average of $1.25 per case to their billing price. That extra gave us an advertising appropriation. I was sure that extra price would not reduce the sale, in view of our advertising efforts. And it gave us a fund to develop new users.

I went to the plants where these puffed grains were made. Professor A. P. Anderson, the inventor of puffed grains, accompanied me. During nights on the train and days in the factories we studied the possibilities.

I learned the reason for puffing. It exploded every food cell. I proved that it multiplied the grains to eight times normal size. It made every atom available as food.

I watched the process, where the grains were shot from guns. And I coined the phrase, "Foods shot from guns."

That idea aroused ridicule. One of the greatest food advertisers in the country wrote an article about it. He said that of all the follies evolved in food advertising this certainly was the worst. The idea of appealing to women on a "Food shot from guns" was the theory of an imbecile.

But that theory proved attractive. It aroused curiosity. And that is one of the greatest incentives we know in dealing with human nature.

The theories behind this puffed-grain campaign are worthy of deep consideration. It proved itself the most successful campaign ever conducted on cereals. They made Puffed Wheat and Puffed Rice the largest money-earners in the field of breakfast foods.

First, I established a personality—Professor A. P. Anderson. I have always done that wherever possible. Personalities appeal, while soulless corporations do not. Make a man famous and you make his creation famous. All of us love to study men and their accomplishments.

Then in every ad I pictured these grains eight times normal size. I made people want to see them.

I told the reason for the puffing. In every grain we created 125,000,000 steam explosions—one for every food cell. Thus all the elements were fitted to digest. I combined every inducement, every appeal which these food products offered.

Puffed grains had been advertised for years, and with increasing disappointment. Advertised as one of countless cereal foods. Nothing was cited to give them particular interest or distinction. The new methods made them unique. They aroused curiosity. No one could read a puffed grain ad without wishing to see those grains. And the test won constant users.

But we made and corrected numerous mistakes. We spent large sums in newspaper advertising, which on that line could not pay. Newspapers reach all the people. This expensive food line appealed only to the classes. Nine in ten whom we reached by newspapers could not afford puffed grains. So we finally proved that magazine advertising was our only possibility.

Then we distributed millions of samples promiscuously. The samples themselves did not win many users. We had to first establish an interest, a respect.

So we stopped giving samples to uninterested people. Then we published ads in tens of millions of magazines, each with a coupon good at any grocery store for a package of Puffed Wheat or Puffed Rice. The people first read our story. If they cut out the coupon, it was because our story had interested. Those people welcomed the package, and they found what they looked for in it.

That is so in all sampling. It never pays to cast samples on the doorstep. They are like waifs. Give samples only to people who take some action to acquire them because of an interest created. Give the product an atmosphere. Otherwise it will never make a lasting impression.

Another thing we learned was this: We published tens of millions of ads which offered Puffed

Wheat free to anyone who bought Puffed Rice. The offer was ineffective, as all such offers are. It meant simply a price reduction. It is just as hard to sell at a half price as at a full price to people not converted. All our millions of ads. on those lines brought us few new users.

So advertisers always find it. A coupon good for half the price is small inducement. A coupon which requires ten cents for a sample appeals to a small percentage. Remember that you are the seller. You are trying to win customers. Then make a trial easy to the people whom you interest. Don't ask them to pay for your efforts to sell them.

Economy on this point multiplies the cost of selling. Inquiries for free samples may cost 25 cents each. Ask 10 cents for the sample, and the inquiries may cost you $1.25 or more. To gain that 10 cents you may be losing one dollar. And you may start only one-fifth as many users for the money that you spend. That is one of the greatest follies in advertising.

My success on puffed grains led the Quaker Oats Company to ask me to study their other propositions. The main one was Quaker Oats. There I made one of the greatest mistakes of my life.

I figured that The Quaker Oats Company controlled a large percentage of the oatmeal business. If we could increase the consumption of oatmeal, we would reap most of the benefits. So I planned my first campaign on those lines.

I shall not describe the methods. They were far-reaching and effective, so far as they could go. I employed hundreds of men to gather data for me, but I was wrong. The eating of oatmeal has for centuries been regarded as important. Everybody knows the value of oatmeal. Those who do not employ it have a reason hard to overcome.

I ran an educational campaign on a new and appealing line. But it did not pay. We found that converting new users was a very expensive proposal. No new user would pay us in his lifetime the cost of his conversion.

That is so in many lines. For instance, converting people to the tooth brush to secure new tooth paste users. New converts, I figure, cost at least $25. No tooth-paste maker could get that cost back in decades.

New habits are created by general education. They are created largely by writers who occupy free space. I have never known of a line where individual advertisers could profitably change habits.

If that cannot be done on a big scale, it certainly cannot be done on a small scale. Every line, every word, directed to that end is a waste. No one can profitably change habits in paid print. The advertiser comes in when those habits are changed. He says: "Here is the right method."

Many millions of dollars have been wasted by advertisers who do not recognize that fact. They aim at people not yet schooled to use the products which they offer. The idea is fine and altruistic, but it never can be made to pay.

All my later advertising on Quaker Oats was aimed at oatmeal users. I never tried to win new users. I simply told existing users the advantages we offered. And we gained large results on those lines.

Our greatest results came during the war, when all of us were urged to meat substitutes, when the study of calories became a fad. The calories in Quaker Oats showed conspicuously. The cost per 1,000 calories was about one-tenth the cost of meat. We doubled the Quaker Oats sales on that calorie presentation.

But we always had in mind that the use of oatmeal was retarded by long cooking. A competitor came out with oats which cooked quickly, and he made vast inroads on our sales. Just then an inventor came to us with the idea of ready-cooked oats. We called them Two-minute Oats. All they required was the heating.

We considered this a great solution of the oatmeal problem. Most of us wanted to adopt it without tests. But I urged experiments.

So we tried Two-minute Oats in a few towns. We offered a package free. Then we wrote to the users and asked their opinion. The verdict was against us. The flavor was different from oatmeal as they knew it. New users might consider it a better flavor. They probably would. But the regular users of oatmeal rebelled at the change, and new users were too few to consider.

So Two-minute Oats proved a failure.

Later came the idea of oats that cooked in from three to five minutes. The flavor was not unique. Most of the directors voted against it because Two-minute Oats had failed. But I urged them to make a test. Learn what the housewives said. We named it Quick Quaker Oats.

So we made a test in a few towns. We offered to buy the first package to try. We told every user we did not care whether they preferred Quaker Oats or Quick Quaker. All we wanted to know was their preference. Some 90 per cent of those users voted for Quick Quaker. And now Quick Quaker gives to Quaker Oats a decided advantage.

All of which teaches us lessons of vast importance. Our success depends on pleasing people. By an inexpensive test we can learn if we please them or not. We can guide our endeavors accordingly.

Two-minute Oats failed because the unique flavor did not appeal to most people. But Quick Quaker gave to the Quaker Oats Company a new hold on the oatmeal business. The difference was decided by submitting the question to a few thousand housewives at small expense. That can always be done. One can always learn what is wanted and what is not wanted, without any considerable risk.

That is about the only way to advertising success. Perhaps one time in fifty a guess may be right. But fifty times in fifty an actual test tells you what to do and avoid.

Chapter Fourteen

Pepsodent

The greatest success of my career so far has been made on Pepsodent Tooth Paste. Its promoter has been associated with me for twenty-two years. We have made millions together in advertising enterprises. When I went with Lord & Thomas he was quite despondent. He offered me a large salary to idle and wait for him to find some mutual opportunity.

He became involved in irrigation projects in Tucson, Arizona. There the nights are long and lonesomeness omnipotent. So he courted the acquaintance of the health-seekers there, and one of them had evolved this tooth paste.

When he brought it to me I tried to discourage him. It was a technical proposition. I did not see a way to educate the laity in technical tooth-paste theories. He insisted on a fifty-cent price, when twenty-five cents had been the usual price for a tooth paste.

But he was persistent. So I finally agreed to undertake the campaign if he gave me a six months' option on a block of stock, which he did.

I read book after book by dental authorities on the theory on which Pepsodent was based. It was dry reading. But in the middle of one book I found a reference to the mucin plaques on teeth, which I afterward called the film. That gave me an appealing idea.

I resolved to advertise this tooth paste as a creator of beauty. To deal with that cloudy film.

The natural idea in respect to a tooth paste is to make it a preventive. But my long experience had taught me that preventive measures were not popular. People will do anything to cure a trouble, but little to prevent it. Countless advertising ideas have been wrecked by not understanding that phase of human nature. Prevention offers slight appeal to humanity in general.

Then I was urged to present the results of neglect, the negative side of the subject. But I had learned that repulsive ideas seldom won readers or converts. People do not want to read of the penalties. They want to be told of rewards. "Laugh and the world laughs with you, weep and you weep alone." People want to be told the ways to happiness and cheer.

This point is important. Every advertising campaign depends on its psychology. Success or failure is determined by the right or wrong appeal. Scores have tried to scare people into using a certain tooth paste. Not one has succeeded, so far as I know, save where they appealed to troubles already created. Folks give little thought to warding off disasters. Their main ambition is to attain more success, more happiness, more beauty, more cheer.

I recognized that fundamental. I never referred to disasters. I never pictured the afflicted. Every illustration I ever used showed attractive people and beautiful teeth.

But there were many more things to consider. Some I had learned by previous experience, some I had to learn in this line. We keyed every ad. by the coupon. We tried out hundreds of ads. Week by week the results were reported to me, and with each report came the headline we employed. Thus I gradually learned the headlines that appealed and the headlines which fell flat.

I learned that beauty was the chief appeal. Most men and women desired to be attractive. When I could offer a convincing way they listened to my arguments. So I came to feature beauty.

But I learned something else. The man who argues for his own advantage is usually disregarded, often scorned. This is particularly true on any subject pertaining to hygiene.

When I urged any person to buy Pepsodent, I was met with apathy. When I asked them to send ten cents for a sample, they almost ignored me. So I was forced to altruistic advertising. The sample was free. The whole object of the ad. was to induce a test for the good of the parties concerned. I never even mentioned that Pepsodent was for sale. I never quoted its price. My whole apparent object was to prove at our cost what Pepsodent could do.

This line brought another revelation. In most lines, like food products, the word "free" was appealing. It multiplied the readers of our ads. The offer of a sample seemed a natural way to sell.

But when we came to something pertaining to hygiene the psychology was different. We were professing to offer people benefits of vast importance. When we featured a gift, like a breakfast food, it minimized our importance. It made us traders, simply seeking to sell, not scientists seeking to benefit. When we featured a free offer at the top of our ads. we divided our results by four.

Such things are not easy to discover. When we advertise a dessert and feature a free package, it harmonizes with human nature. When we offer a hygienic help and make the word "free" a chief appeal, we discredit all the factors which can bring us converts.

I spent much time to learn this. I wasted some money. But I always knew immediately, by my keyed coupons, the effects of my every appeal. I learned my mistakes in a week. I never spent much money on any wrong theory. I discovered quickly the right and the wrong.

Here we are dealing with one of the greatest successes in advertising. A tooth paste which, despite all opposition, came to rule the world. Today it is sold in 52 countries. It is advertised in 17 languages, including the Chinese, and in each our appeal has proved equally effective.

We came into a field well occupied. During all of our advancement we had countless competitors. We won over them all and made Pepsodent, in a few short years, the star dentifrice success. This was no accident.

The Pepsodent Company was organized on a small capital. Most of the investment went into office fixtures and machinery. All men connected were old advertisers. They would never have invested much in trade creating without assurance of quick return.

We secured that quick return. In our first test city we spent $1,000, which came back with a profit before the advertising bills were due. We tried other cities, and they panned out in like way. Then our backers advanced large sums of money on a plan that had proved a certainty. Thus we established in one year a nation-wide demand, and a world-wide demand in four years.

Consider this undertaking. I know of nothing in all advertising so successful in a big, quick way. One series of ads which I prepared would have wrecked it in three months. Yet I had at that time spent nearly thirty years in advertising. I had learned from hundreds of campaigns.

I caught my mistakes by the coupon—caught them quickly. I reversed my strategy at once. Before we went very far, I had found the way to quick and sure success, simply by watching returns.

A hundred tooth-paste makers might start out, as a hundred have, and fall down. Simply because they were wedded to some theory which human nature failed to approve. They did not learn their mistake, because they did not quickly check results. So they wrecked themselves on rocks which could have been avoided.

I made for myself a million dollars on Pepsodent —on a proposition which at first I refused to undertake. Just because by countless tests I learned the right human psychology.

What is the lesson? It is that none of us can afford to rely on judgment or experience. We must feel our way. New problems require new experience. We must test our undertakings in the most exact way possible. Learn our mistakes and correct them. Watch every appealing lead.

After this experience, I can cite a hundred ways to advertise a tooth paste wrongly. And I can prove the mistakes. But a hundred men might follow each to the rocks if they had no gauge on results. A hundred men have done so. So Pepsodent offers the best argument I know for being guided by actual data.

Chapter Fifteen

Some
mail-order experiences

Most of my advertising accounts were developed along the lines here described. To go into details would be monotonous. But all my life I have done a certain percentage of mail-order advertising. It is not profitable from an agency standpoint. It is difficult and time-consuming, and it seldom runs to large amounts. But it is educational. It keeps one on his mettle. It fixes one's viewpoint on cost and result. The ad.-writer learns more from mail-order advertising than from any other form.

So far as possible, in all my ad.-writing, I make successful mail-order advertising my model and my guide. That is proved advertising. It is known to be profitable, else it would not continue. It is usually the result of many traced experiments, so it represents the best advertising yet found for that line.

Mail-order advertising is a profitable study. Note its economy of space. It is nearly always set in small type. That is because thousands of tests have proved larger type wasteful. All pictures have a selling value. None are used for decoration.

Take a profitable mail-order ad. and set it in twice the space. Use larger type, more decorations or a border. You will get an ad. which looks more attractive, but you will double the cost of replies and sales.

This fact should be accepted, for this economy principle, after thousands of tests on hundreds of lines, has become practically universal. And it proves that waste of space is folly in any line of advertising. That includes large type, or borders, or pictures that don't help to sell. All ads. would be set like good mail-order ads. if the same rigid tests were applied.

That is the hardest fact for an ad.-writer to learn or an advertiser to comprehend. The natural instinct is to make the ad. attractive. One must remember, however, ads. are not written to amuse, but to sell. And to sell at the lowest cost possible. Mail-order advertising, based on accurate figures on cost and result, shows the best ways known to do that.

An advertiser who once came to our agency was selling a five-dollar article by mail. His replies were costing 85 cents each, his sales about $2.50 each. The advertising was becoming unprofitable, so he sought a way to lessen cost of sales. We prepared an ad. which the advertiser rejected, it seemed so unattractive. Another agency prepared a larger, more alluring ad., which the advertiser tried. But his cost per reply was $14.20, on an article which sold for $5. Then he tried our ad., and the cost per reply was 42 cents. So we secured the advertising, and our cost per reply kept around 42 cents for years. We cut his old cost in two. And that, on 250,000 replies per year, meant a very big item to him. But countless advertisers without a trace on cost are judging ads. by appearance. And they are losing as heavily as this man did on an ad. which cost him $14.20 per reply. That is why so much money is wasted in advertising. People do not know their costs, and they will not be guided by those who do. So I have always done some mail-order advertising to help me keep my feet on the ground.

At one time I took up the advertising of house-furnishings by mail on installments. While I was doing this the business developed to $7,000,000 per year. That taught me countless things. One learns a great deal about human nature in selling goods on credit by mail.

The problem does not end with the first sale to a customer. The catalogs are expensive. Landing a customer in this line costs money. A percentage of the customers fail to pay as agreed. So profit depends on making the most of customers who are honest. Selling them again and again. Mailing bulletins on special offers. Watching accounts to sell something more when payments are completed. Inducing one customer to interest others.

One day when I called on this concern I noted a big building next door. I asked about it, and they told me it belonged to a firm that sold women's garments by mail on installments, just as we sold furnishings. I said: "Why do you let such a concern grow up next to you? Why don't you sell their line?"

That led us to organize a similar concern. I urged them to give it a woman's name. We selected a capable, middle-aged woman and pictured her in every ad. We had her sign the ads., and we made our appeal from one woman to another.

These ads. did not mention installments. They dealt with the subject of credit. They appealed to young women who desired to appear at their best. They pointed out what it meant in a woman's career. Then this woman offered to help them out by giving them six months to pay for spring clothes.

The offer was flattering, not humiliating. It showed sympathy and understanding. The evident desire was to serve. In reality our offers were the same as those made by the people next door, but our attitude was different. We made our six months' credit seem like the thirty-day credit which richer women get at their stores.

As a result, we dominated that field from the start. Before long, the business next door was closed. Cold commercialism could not compete with the atmosphere we created. Nor could boasted benefactions appeal like the offer of fair treatment from one woman to another.

Just that change in presentation created an enormous new business. It also led to vastly increased sales on furnishings.

Hundreds of thousands of women flocked to this new line. Most of them paid as agreed and thus established a credit. Then the president of the house-furnishing concern wrote a letter to these women somewhat to this effect: "Today I met Mrs. ___. She told me that you were a customer of hers, that she had sold you on credit and that you had paid as agreed. She says that you are one of her valued customers, and that you are always welcome to buy from her whatever you wish on time.

"I want to make a like offer. We sell house-furnishings here, and I am mailing you our catalog. Disregard the terms in that catalog, which ask for a payment in advance. I am willing to ship you whatever you wish without any advance payment, in view of what Mrs. ___ tells me. Just order what you want. Send no money whatever. Start paying in a month if you find the articles satisfactory, and take your time."

Such an offer was almost irresistible. These women had ordered clothing on credit, wondering if they would get it. They could hardly believe that strangers would trust them. Then the president of a big house-furnishing concern writes that he has opened a credit account because of what the garment-maker told him. They are offered credit on special terms, without any payment in advance. Any woman who receives such a flattering offer will try to find some way to utilize it.

So with the garment-seller. She wrote like letters to the house-furnishing customers. She told them they had with her an open credit account. They could order whatever they wished without sending money. Just order the garments sent on approval. And those house-furnishing customers by the thousands bought women's garments from the woman who wrote them so politely.

We started a like business on men's clothes. Then by making a customer in one line a buyer of another we multiplied the ordinary results. Nobody on a single line could compete with such a combination.

Such are the ramifications of advertising. Salesmanship-in-print, in principle, is just the same as salesmanship-in-person. The store offers a bargain to tempt people there. The object is to try to sell other things, and right salesmanship will do it. An ad.-writer must never forget that he is a simple salesman, and the more he sells the better he will prosper.

One more mail-order experience will illustrate another phase. I took up the advertising of a concern which for thirty years had sold garments for women and children by mail on credit. This field is well occupied. It has been profitable. The annual sales of some concerns in this line run into many millions.

All offer a costly catalog. Some ads. offer special bargains—perhaps certain articles at cost—to induce people to write for the catalog. As a result, the woman who writes for one catalog is apt to write for three or four.

Then comes the main difficulty—the problem of inducing women to buy from your catalog rather than from others.

Say it costs 25 cents to induce a woman to write for your catalog. The catalog, with its pictures in colors, costs 35 cents at least. Thus you have an investment of 60 cents in each inquirer. The results depend on the sale per catalog.

The woman who writes to one advertiser in this line usually writes to three or four. When she comes to make a selection, she has four catalogs before her. All present attractive appeals. The one from which she orders depends largely on chance or fancy.

One must recognize that. Your cost of presenting that catalog to her is 60 cents, perhaps. If four advertisers are presenting such catalogs to her, the total cost is $2.40. The average sale, as per experience, is around $10. So the advertisers combined are spending 25 per cent to make that average sale.

The profit depends on swinging your way more than the average sale. That was the problem which brought those advertisers to me.

I devised this scheme: When a woman wrote for our catalog I went to our card file and discovered whether she was a new or old customer. If she was a new customer, the sales manager wrote her a letter to this effect: "We are very glad to have your inquiry. We welcome new patrons to our fold. I want to extend you that welcome in a practical way. I inclose my card. On it is written instructions to refer your order to me. I want to send with that order, with my compliments, a little present for you. I will not say what it is, but I am sure it will delight you."

To old customers he wrote this: "I am glad to again receive an inquiry from you. The whole profit in our business is made by the customers who stay with us year after year. It costs money to get new customers, but the old ones who remain cost us nothing. So I wish to offer you a token in appreciation of the fact that you continue with us. When you send your order, inclose this card of mine. It instructs our people here to refer your order to me. Then I will include a little gift to show our appreciation."

What was the result? All inquirers for the catalog, old or new customers, received that card. It did not mention the gift, because curiosity makes a stronger appeal than description. But every inquirer had that card before her. If she ordered from one particular catalog she could send that card and receive the gift. So she tried her best to order from that catalog. The sales per catalog were thus enormously increased.

One must be careful in such offers. The gift must not be disappointing. It must be something every woman wants. But any reasonable cost is insignificant if it doubles the sale per catalog. That means doubling the results of the advertising.

All such problems devolve on the advertising man. He may write attractive ads. which gain applause. But if those ads. fail to make sales at a profit, he is wiped out very quickly. He may bring inquiries at small cost, then let rival catalogs outsell him. His usefulness is ended just the same. Business is conducted to make money. A man who can help it make money has boundless possibilities. But the most brilliant efforts which result in loss lead to permanent defeat.

This last line I mention led to another instructive episode. There were six large advertisers in this line of women's garments. Their chief aim was to convince women that they undersold all others.

So they blazoned their claims to low prices. Then they published guaranties to undersell any other prices. Whoever found a better bargain elsewhere could return her purchase.

There came a time when all were crying bargains in the highest key. In a chorus of that kind, all are on the same plane. All are as ineffective as though they made no claims at all.

They presented me the problem of a more impressive claim. I looked up their figures, and I found that their average profit for years past had been less than 3 per cent. So I advertised that profit—a profit of 3 per cent. I promised not to exceed it. We were content with that profit, and our prices were fixed on that basis.

Here was one of the oldest mail-order concerns in this line, one of the largest. The prices they quoted on 3 per cent profit must be pretty close to minimum. One could not expect to materially decrease them. So those quotations, despite all others' guaranties, were accepted as bottom prices.

That is another illustration of how actual figures count. Claims are always discounted. Say, "Lowest prices in existence" and people ignore you. Many may make like claims. But say that you sell at 3 per cent net profit, and most people believe you. They do not expect you to lie in regard to definite figures. They know you cannot lie in the better publications.

Those are some of the plans which I evolved to increase mail-order sales. They meant little to me directly. Mail-order advertising is not worth the effort from the standpoint of the ad -writer. But it kept me facing the fact that all sorts of advertising is based on mail-order principles. We must always sell our goods at a profit. We must always outsell others to succeed. Any ad -writer who proceeds on any other theory is doomed to quick defeat.

Chapter Sixteen

Reasons
for success

Now let me try to summarize the reasons for my success for the benefit of those who will follow. By success I mean the parts I played in developing great advertising enterprises, most of which continue. Advertising men are expected to do that.

In advertising we serve three interests, all of them allied but distinct. First comes the publisher who pays us our commissions. He pays to the agency an average of 15 per cent on the amount of the advertising. That is paid for expected service. The best service we can render lies in the development of new advertising opportunities. He expects us to increase the general volume of advertising by starting new projects or showing the way to profitably increase the old.

Publishers learned that I served them well. I wrote, for instance, the first ad I ever read on automobiles. I did much of the pioneer work in that line, including the first ads on Chalmers, Hudson, and Overland. Publishers regarded me as a leader in that development. The first important tire advertising was the campaign which I evolved on No-Rim-Cut tires for Goodyear. Its amazing success proved to all tire-makers that this line needed advertising.

Tooth-paste advertising was rather insignificant before Pepsodent came into the field. That quick success was one of the marvels of advertising, and now many millions are spent every year to foster dentifrices. No doubt the success of Puffed Wheat and Puffed Rice gave impetus to cereal advertising. The remarkable success of Palmolive created much soap advertising.

My help in creating business for the magazines and newspapers led the publishers to help me. They have opened for me many fine opportunities, just because they believed that my service in ad.-writing would increase their revenues.

Another interest we serve as ad-writers is the advertising agency. Many of the best accounts in agencies are the accounts developed from small beginnings there. Nearly all the accounts I handled were of that sort. Often much is at stake on these advertising possibilities. A mistake may ruin a fine prospect. Mediocre service may result in a small account where a big one might have been. That is why competent ad -writers are paid such large incomes.

In my case I started with Lord & Thomas at $1,000 per week. But we soon agreed that the right plan was a commission basis. Then the agency paid me only for service which proved profitable to them. On the other hand, I received what I earned. Under that plan I earned in commissions as high as $185,000 in a year. All earned at a typewriter which I operated myself, without a clerk or secretary, and much of it earned in the woods. In addition I received a number of valuable interests, some of them without cost, in the enterprises I helped to develop.

My commission grew until it became one-third the whole agency commission. Mr. Lasker, during all my years with him, let me write my own contracts. He sometimes signed them without reading, for he believed me fair. But the natural result was that no accounts were turned over to me which other men could handle. Most of my accounts were developments from little test campaigns.

But I was doing more than serve myself. I was doing my best to teach other copy men in the agency. I held many meetings with them to discuss the principles of copy. For that I received no pay. Then I wrote numerous books to set down the agency principles.

Because of those services Mr. Lasker finally made me president of Lord & Thomas. Then, for certain reasons, chairman of the board. When he went to Washington to serve President Harding as chairman of the Shipping Board I served for two more years as president of the agency. Those two years cost me considerable money. My commissions dropped because of my other duties. I received no salary as president, yet I spent much time with new clients. I presided at a meeting of our leading men every morning to help all our men who had problems. During those two years I accepted no account for myself. By that I mean an account on which I obtained commissions. I wanted no one to say that I used my position to secure revenue for myself. As a result, my own revenue dropped severely. But Mr. Lasker always knew that his interests would come ahead of mine. He trusted me implicitly. At one time, to help compensate, he gave me a check for $10,000 for writing *Scientific Advertising*.

That was one great factor in my career—the confidence I engendered. That was due to my Scotch ancestry. At one time Mr. Lasker made me a trustee under his will. Again and again I refused to accept from him more than I felt I earned. When my contract called for one-third the commission I refused to accept it on accounts where I did not appear to be a vital factor. About the only disagreements I had with Mr. Lasker referred to his desire to overpay me.

That attitude I consider a vital factor in success. An absolutely fair division. One on the crest of the wave may over-play his hand for a little time, but not for long. Business is money-making, and associates will find a way to eliminate anyone who claims too large a share.

The third element in advertising is the advertiser himself. I put him third because he seems to come third in my conception of advertising. We cannot serve the publisher or the advertising agent without serving him. But the publisher pays our commissions, the advertising agent selects and employs us. The advertiser who is a beginner makes a slight speculation on us. Old advertisers who change from one agency to another are not very valuable clients. They have failed in their ambitions. In a large percentage of cases the reason for failure cannot be corrected. So they usually switch again.

The advertisers I value most are not those who come with large appropriations. I could list scores of such advertisers who have no prospect of attaining their desires. Each succeeding agent loses reputation and prestige when he attempts the impossible.

The most valuable clients are those who come to us with new opportunities in advertising. They are many. But the opportunity consists of a test campaign, costing under $5,000. The agency commission on such a campaign is $750. The cost of developing a test campaign rarely runs under $20,000 if a competent man is employed. The men in charge may spend weeks in reading and in research.

The stake in such cases is largely with the agency. The advertiser usually gets his money back, whatever the outcome. The real stake is made by the agency.

Failure means that the advertiser loses a trifle, the agency loses much. Success may mean millions to the advertiser. To the agency it means 15 per cent commission on the advertising just so long as he holds the advertiser's good will and approval. So I feel no obligation to an advertiser who permits me to make a test. Mine is the speculation.

That is why I place advertisers last in this category. But on the success of the advertiser depends everything else. We owe obligation to the publishers who pay us our commissions. We owe obligation to the agency which gives us our chance. Our least obligation is to the advertiser, yet everything depends on his attitude.

Success in advertising depends on these three elements. Three interests must be satisfied, and all of them are crying for profits. The only way to please all of them is to profitably develop what you undertake.

I have devoted myself to the advertiser. Through his success must come my success with the others. I forget the rest. The advertiser who fails in a large way becomes forever a denouncer of advertising. I know that failure is inevitable in a large

percentage of cases. So I never involve the adventurer to any large extent before we are sure
of a profit. If he fails, the fault lies in the product
or conditions, not the advertising. His loss is little
or nothing. If he succeeds, his winnings may run
into millions.

How have I been able to win from this situation
so many great successes? Simply because I made
so many mistakes in a small way, and learned something from each. I made no mistake twice. Every
once in a while I developed some great advertising
principle. That endured.

That method cost me, beginning as I did in the
infancy of advertising, an enormous amount of
time. More time than other men are apt to devote
to this primitive experience. Much more time,
much more sacrifice, than I would want a son of
mine to devote. That is the purpose of this autobiography. To help other men to start where I
ended.

Mr. A. D. Lasker, who is a very wise man, often
attributed much of my success to living among
simple people. He always wanted me to work in
the woods where I write this history, and I have
done so for two decades. Here most of the people
I talk with are my gardeners, their families, and
the village folk near by. I learn what they buy
and their reasons for buying. Those reasons would
surprise many who gain their impressions from
golf-club associates.

The reason is rarely economy. We hear people of large incomes boast of their economies. They are not humiliated by them. But where economy is a necessity most people like to defy it. When silk shirts cost $15 they became so common among laboring men that other classes went to broadcloth. Every shopgirl demands silk stockings. My experience on cosmetics proves that a low price on perfumes, etc., does not appeal to the girl who should economize. She demands what the "best people" use.

Many people around me, working at small wages, consider cost far less than I do. A woman who does our washing, and who arrives in her own car, has a fad for antiques. She picks up many pieces of value—pieces we are glad to buy from her when she becomes involved.

The proudest people I know are the people who work on my country place. Suggest a thing to them because it is economical and you arouse opposition. You hurt their pride. But direct your appeal to those who do not consider cost and they like to be included.

That is a single example of the things we learn by contact from the people who form 95 per cent of our customers. America is a land of equality.

Every campaign that I devise or write is aimed at some individual member of this vast majority. I do not consult managers and boards of directors. Their viewpoint is nearly always distorted. I

Chapter Seventeen

Scientific advertising

Through a book I wrote my name has become connected with "Scientific Advertising." That is, advertising based on fixed principles and done according to fundamental laws. I learned those principles through thirty-six years of traced advertising. Through conducting campaigns on some hundreds of different lines. Through comparing on some lines, by keyed returns, thousands of pieces of copy. Always, since I sent out my first thousand letters to the time when $5,000,000 yearly was being spent on my copy, I have had to face records on cost and result. So I have naturally proved out many fundamentals which should always be applied.

I have little respect for most theories of advertising, because they have not been proved. They are based on limited experiences, on exceptional conditions. Some lines seem to succeed on methods of advertising which every traced return proves impossible. The reasons for success have little to do with the advertising. The line may have succeeded in spite of the advertising. Many unadvertised lines become highly successful, because of some wanted quality which people soon discover. Or because dealers are in some way induced to feature it. Or because of a name which in itself tells an appealing story.

Cream of Wheat is an example. The name alone tells the story. So with Spearmint Gum. All successful gums have succeeded through fortunate names. There is almost no story to tell. There are no great distinctions. The very men who succeeded with one name failed again and again with others.

Any conclusions drawn from such experiences are bound to lead others astray. The cases where they apply are rare. Safe principles are evolved only by those who know with reasonable exactness what the advertising does, and who compare results on many lines with thousands of pieces of copy. Mail-order advertising gives the most exact basis, but most advertising can be so conducted as to give an approximate guide.

To apply scientific advertising one must recognize that ads are salesmen. One must compare them, one by one, on a salesman's basis, and hold them responsible for cost and result. To advertise blindly teaches one nothing, and it usually leads to the rocks.

I have described in this book some of the methods by which we trace results. But we find that some methods which succeed in one line cannot be applied to another. We find that some methods which are profitable are not one-fourth so effective as others. So, regardless of principles, we must always experiment. But there are certain basic laws so well established, so generally accepted by those who know returns, that all who are wise will recognize and generally employ them. I intend in this chapter to deal with such principles only.

Brilliant writing has no place in advertising. A unique style takes attention from the subject. Any apparent effort to sell creates corresponding resistance. Persuasive ability arouses the fear of over-influence. Anything which suggests an effort to sell on other lines than merit and service is fatal.

One should be natural and simple. His language should not be conspicuous. In fishing for buyers, as in fishing for bass, one should not reveal the hook.

Never try to show off. You are selling your product, not yourself. Do nothing to cloud your objective. Use the shortest words possible. Let every phrase ring with sincerity.

From start to finish offer service. That is what you are selling, that is all your prospect wants. Weigh every sentence on that basis. Waste no space, no money to any other end. I have seen many an ad killed by a single unfortunate phrase. Usually a selfish phrase, indicating ulterior desires which repel. Phrases like "Insist on this brand," "Avoid imitations," "Look out for substitution." Such appeals have no good effect, and they indicate a motive with which buyers cannot sympathize.

Forget yourself entirely. Have in your mind a typical prospect, interested enough to read about your product. Keep that prospect before you. Seek in every word to increase your good impression. Say only what you think a good salesman should say if that prospect stood before him. Then, if you could sell in person, you could sell in print.

Do not boast. Not about your plant or your output. Not about anything more interesting to you than to your prospect. Boasting is repulsive.

Aim to get action. Your reader is perusing a magazine or newspaper. She has paused because your subject or your headline attracts her. But in a moment she will be interested in her reading and will usually forget you. In some way in your climax inspire immediate action in those interested. A coupon is the usual way. People cut it out. They do not lay aside their magazine or newspaper, but they clip the coupon to remind them of something they decide to do. A woman lays it on her desk, a man slips it in his vest pocket. Then on some convenient occasion it turns up for action. It is sent in for a sample or for further information. Then you have a chance to follow up that interest.

Countless tests have proved that coupons multiply returns. I have seen many tests made by mail-
order houses, offering catalogs. Some ads. had
coupons; some did not. The difference in returns
was enormous.

People are dilatory. They defer action, then forget. Many an advertiser loses in that way most
of his half-made converts. One cannot afford that.

There are other ways to get action. The "week"
sales have that in view. The retail offers which
apply to a certain day or hour. Limited offers of
every sort. Something to induce prompt action,
to avoid procrastination, is always an important
factor.

Frivolity has no place in advertising. Nor has
humor. Spending money is usually serious business.
This does not apply to amusement advertising, but
it does to all other forms. Money represents life
and work. It is highly respected. To most people,
spending money in one direction means skimping
in another. So money-spending usually has a serious purpose. People want full value. They want
something worth more to them than the same
amount spent in other ways would buy.

Such subjects should not be treated lightly. No
writer who really knows the average person will
ever treat it lightly. Money comes slowly and by
sacrifice. Few people have enough. The average person is constantly choosing between one way to spend
and another. Appeal for money in a lightsome

way and you will never get it. "Sunny Jim" proved that, so did "Spotless Town." So did many others which are long forgotten. Nobody can cite a permanent success built on frivolity. People do not buy from clowns.

Never seek to amuse. That is not the purpose of advertising. People get their amusements in the reading-matter columns. The only interest you can offer profitably is something people want.

Do not try to compete with the stories or the news columns, with the pictures or the cartoons in their field. You may win attention, but not valuable attention. Most of the people you attract in this way have no interest in your subject.

The ad -columns and the reading matter have their separate purposes. You cannot fool people by any resemblance. None should attempt it if he could. What does it profit an advertiser to attract a reader who has no interest in his subject? Any product worth advertising, if rightly presented, has more interest than a story. It means economy, or help, or pleasure—perhaps for years to come. Amusement is transient. Why sacrifice your great appeal to secure a moment's fickle attention?

Advertising means salesmanship to millions. Because of its big field it is very expensive. In national advertising the average cost is at least $10 per word. One must figure that. Make every word count to the limit. Cut out every word which is not worth that $10. Never repeat. This should be done without stilted effects, but it must be done.

A salesman who wastes his time, who says useless things and repeats, may cost $1 per hour. But an ad. which does like things is wasting $10 per word. And such wastes are important. The difference between profit and loss in advertising is not usually very great. If success were easy, the field would be overcrowded. Most success comes through efficiency. Most failures are due to waste.

Do not waste space in any way. It is expensive. Remember that all our ordinary reading is done in 8-point type. Most mail-order advertisers, presenting something more interesting than ordinary reading matter, have adopted 6-point type. Despite these facts, countless advertisers present their story in larger type. I do not know the theory. Certainly the easiest type to read is the ordinary. Anything unusual presents to us difficulties.

Advertisers struggle for attention. They strive to demand it, not induce it. And big type is one of their methods. Anyone who traces results can quickly prove that oversize type does not pay. Double your necessary space and you double your cost. All mail-order advertising proves that, as do all other forms of traced advertising. If your story is interesting, people will read it in their accustomed types. If it isn't interesting, they will read it in no size of type. Or, if they do, their reading will not help you.

On the same theory, many put their display lines in all caps. They think they look more prominent. But all our reading is done in upper-and-lower case type. We are accustomed to that. When we meet lines set in capitals, we have to study them out. This may not be a severe handicap, but it is always a detriment. Why not follow the usual and natural?

Then comes the principles connected with art in advertising. The inclination is to use pictures. The tendency has grown until many advertisers pay from $1,500 to $4,000 per drawing.

No test that I know of proves such expense profitable. Nor do I know of a case where colored pictures paid better than black-and-white. People use them more and more, but rarely on traced advertising.

I am prepared to believe that on some lines, like fruits and desserts, colored pictures may prove profitable. But I know of no line as yet where, on traced returns, they have warranted their extra cost. And I have made a good many comparisons. At one time a great advertising journal appealed for proofs that colored advertising paid. But no such actual proof has yet come to my attention.

That is a question for further experiment. Extra-fine art work and colored art work have not yet proved their advantages. If they do so in certain lines, I doubt if ever the results can be applied to all lines.

The incentive is not allied to salesmanship. One cares little how a salesman dresses. We regard over-dress as a fault. So with salesmanship-in-print. I have never found a case where fine appearance paid its cost in extra sales. And I know of no one else who has done so. My idea is that fine art work, like fine language, simply makes buyers wary.

Another principle taught by experience is that ads. should tell the full story. People do not read ads. in series. The advertiser who today attracts them may not again get attention for months. So, when you get a reading, present all your arguments. In an advertising campaign, we find facts which appeal, and we retain them. We find other facts which don't appeal, and we drop them. We find these things out by featuring our various claims in headlines. We find that one lead brings a great deal of interest, while another brings little or none. So we gauge our appeals accordingly.

Some will buy for one reason, some for another. But all appeals which prove themselves important should be included in every ad. Otherwise, our most convincing arguments fail to reach our in-terested readers.

We cannot expect people to read our ads. again and again. Our subject attracts them, and they give us brief attention. It is up to us, then, to con-vince them or forever lose their interest. They will not read another ad. of ours if we fail to present in an enticing way something they desire.

We should not lose our opportunity. Every ad should include whatever we have found appealing to any considerable class.

Then there are different ways of stating things. Some are impressive, some are not. Superlative claims do not count. To say that something is "The best in the world" makes no impression whatever. That is an expected claim. The reader may not blame us for exaggeration, but we lose much of his respect. He naturally minimizes whatever else we may say.

When we say such things as, "The best product in existence," "The supreme creation of its kind," we may arouse only a smile at our frailties. No resentment may be engendered. But whatever else we say is discounted.

People are pretty well educated to the belief that advertising must tell the truth. They know that we cannot, in the better mediums, deliberately mislead them. But they do not regard superlatives as misleading, because they never are.

On the other hand, when you state actual figures, definite facts, they accept them at par. Such definite statements are either facts or lies, and people do not expect that reputable people or concerns will lie.

Give actual figures, state definite facts. Take the tungsten lamp as an example. Say that it gives more light than other lamps, and people are but mildly impressed. Say that it gives $3\frac{1}{3}$ times the light of carbon lamps, and people will realize that you have made actual comparisons. They will accept your claims at par.

So in everything. Indefinite claims leave indefinite impressions, and most of them are weak. But definite claims get full credit and value. The reader must either decide you correct or decide that you are lying. And the latter supposition is unusual.

Never advertise negatively. Always present the attractive side, not the offensive side of a subject. Do not picture or feature ills. The people you appeal to have enough. Show and feature the happier results which come from your products or methods.

People are seeking happiness, safety, beauty, and content. Then show them the way. Picture happy people, not the unfortunate. Tell of what comes from right methods, not what results from the wrong. For instance, no tooth-paste manufacturer ever made an impression by picturing dingy teeth. Or by talking decay and pyorrhea. The successes have been made by featuring the attractive sides.

All experience in advertising proves that people will do little to prevent troubles. They do not cross bridges in advance. They will do anything to cure troubles which exist, but legitimate advertising has little scope there. All are seeking advantages, improvements, new ways to satisfy desires. They are not inclined to anticipate disasters. Those who have met misfortune form in most lines a percentage too small to consider.

There are many things in advertising too costly to attempt. One must avoid them, else he will become disheartened. An ointment, for instance, or a germicide, a treatment for asthma or hay fever, a rub for rheumatism.

On some such things one appeals to a small percentage. The cost of reaching them in mediums of universal circulation is excessive. It cannot come back for decades. On others, the cost of securing a customer is many years' return from a customer. Repeat sales are too far apart.

I know many products which every home should have. The reasons are convincing. A large percentage of homes can be sold on them, but a single purchase lasts for months and sometimes years. The cost of securing a customer far exceeds the first-sale profit. Further sales and profits are long deferred. The advertiser and the advertising man become discouraged long before the tide can turn.

The world is full of such things. Things that appeal to the 1 per cent. Things that do not repeat until funds and patience are exhausted. I have seen many men of great ability discouraged by such undertakings.

Another thing to learn exactly is what sort of headline most appeals. Again and again I have multiplied results from an ad. by eight or ten by a simple change in headline.

A headline is intended to salute the people you desire to reach. It is just like a bell-boy in a hotel calling for Mr. Jones. Here is a message for him. Or like the heading on a news article. All of us depend on headlines to point out what we desire to read.

Consider your ordinary readers. You have presented to you, perhaps a hundred times what you have time to peruse. You select your reading by the headings. So it is in ads.

We must discover what appeals are most impressive. We learn that by keyed tests, by comparing one headline with another. We find that one sort of headline appeals to 25 per cent of our prospects, and another to 50 per cent. We must use them accordingly.

Any other method involves tremendous waste. Anyone can quickly prove that if he uses keyed returns. Good ads. on any line cannot vary greatly. They must be complete, and completeness means similarity. The great difference lies in the headline. One attracts a certain percentage, another ten times as many. One must find that out if he expects his advertising to appeal to a profitable audience.

One person presents a subject in a way to flatter, another in a way to humiliate. One bases his claims on self-interest, another on service. One tries to sell, another tries to please. These things all alter one's attitude of mind, and that is what leads to decision.

But psychology goes further. It recognizes pride and individuality. One must know how to appeal to those desires. These things can hardly be taught. They come through kindly instincts, through love and understanding, through desires to please and serve. No man out of tune with his fellows can be taught them.

The best school I know is canvassing, going from home to home. Many great ad.-writers spend half their time in that. They learn by personal contacts what wins and what repulses. Then they apply their findings to appeals in print.

These factors must all be considered. They form the foundation of advertising. Suppose it were different. Anyone who can write a fair letter can write a fair ad. Suppose that ordinary presentations, without regard to the subject, could sell lines at a profit. There would be no room in ad.-writing for men of ambition.

But such things can't be done. The line is fiercely competitive. Every ad. is surrounded by countless appeals. Every effort involves much expense. The man who wins out and survives does so only because of superior science and strategy. He must know more, must be better grounded, must be shrewder than his rivals. The only way to that end is to start with fixed principles, proved by decades of experience, from which you never swerve.

Chapter Eighteen

My
great mistake

The day before Christmas, in the year I made my initial success in selling carpet sweepers by letters, Mr. M. R. Bissell, president of the company, called me to his office. He said: "I have some advice to give you. You have many of the qualifications which make for success, including the selling instinct. You are too good a man to work for me. You shall start out for yourself, as I did."

He told me something of his history. How he had refused every salary offer, every safe anchorage, and struggled alone. And how as a result he had finally arrived on the road to fortune.

He ended by saying: "I am selfish enough to want you to stay here. If you do, your salary will be much increased next year. But I am fair enough to advise you not to stay. Don't let some one else glean the chief profits from your hard work and your talent."

My Scotch conservatism led me to stay. It was my great mistake. Soon after that I married, and any venture of my own became increasingly difficult. Thus I tied myself to a lifetime of service as an employee.

I watched some of my coworkers start out for themselves, largely on lines I had taught them. Fred Macey started selling furniture by mail. In a few months he had an office force of ninety to handle the business he developed. Then he founded the Fred Macey Company which exists today. A. W. Shaw started building office systems. Then he founded the magazine *System*, which has been an enormous success. My roommate, E. H. Stafford, left his position to manufacture school furniture, and built up the E. H. Stafford Company. I feel now, as then, that I was fully as well equipped as they were, save with courage. I have been called on to do bigger things for others than they have done for themselves. But I always envied their independence which I spent thirty-five years to attain.

I have helped a good many men to wealth and position. In many cases—in most cases—they started practically without money. The advertising had to earn its way. It was the chief factor in the business, often the only reason for success. In most mail-order lines that is evident. It is true in

many other lines. It is not difficult to make a breakfast food, a tooth paste, medicine, soap, or cleanser.
Most advertisers at the start employ others to
make them. Salesmen can aid but little. They are
usually not employed. About everything depends
on the advertising.

I have told how such products are tested out,
in a small way at the start. The advertising man
does nine-tenths of the work. The owner of the
trade-mark ventures little or nothing. If the test
falls down, the advertising man is the main loser.
He has spent his time and talents. If the test succeeds and the advertising extends, the advertising man gets a commission on the expenditures.
The profits go to others. The advertising man, because he is anonymous, fails to even get due credit.

The business grows, and the owners grow with
it, in wealth and in pride. As it grows, the advertising man becomes less and less important. The
business acquires a momentum. The time comes
when even mediocre advertising will keep it going
upward. Advertising which could never have
started it.

The advertising man clings to the methods he
established. He fears to change. As a matter of
fact, it is seldom wise to change. The best way to
win new customers is usually the way that won
millions. But the advertising becomes monotonous
to the men who read every ad. They always come
to want something new. So the man who builds a

big advertising account is pretty sure to lose it, soon or late. To keep up his volume and his earnings he must always be starting new ventures.

I gradually came to specialize on proprietaries and foods, on products which people buy over and over. They offer the great opportunities in advertising. One-sale articles are not so inviting. The profit must be made on that sale. Articles of that kind appeal to the minority. The advertising man's great profits come from products which appeal to nearly every home, and which must be advertised forever. Food products, for instance, which mothers teach their children to use, and which never should go out of favor.

But such products must be developed. The process is often slow. The advertising man has the major share of the work and responsibility. When he works for others, as I worked for thirty-five years, he gets no fair share of the profits. And he rarely becomes a permanent factor, so far as his work is concerned.

I have often figured what I would have made had I invested just my commissions in the stock of enterprises which I fostered. The amount runs into many millions. The real reason I did not is the fact that I never had sufficient confidence in myself. But I pretended to ignore commercialism. My creative work lay in a higher sphere. So for many years I watched others make money, while I gained mainly a modicum of fame.

An ambitious wife was the one who woke me from that lethargy. She had desires for which money counted more than fame. She pointed out how those who employed me always gained the advantage in a monetary way.

Finally I considered her viewpoint, and after many years of working for others I started to work for myself. I have already made more by sharing the profits of my creations than I ever made by working on commission.

One of my first ventures was in Pepsodent tooth paste. I bought a share in that, for which I paid $13,000. It paid me some $200,000 in dividends, then I sold the stock for $500,000.

Then I decided, at a time in life when most men wish to retire, that I would do what Mr. Bissell advised me to do when I was twenty-one. I would work for myself, start my own enterprises, and win or fail with them.

I had many ideas in mind. The first one I started was a cosmetic business. I had studied statistics on that line. I learned that women spent $700,000,000 yearly on cosmetics—more than they spent on all other advertised lines combined. I prepared a line of cosmetics, but I had no theory. The field was overcrowded. Leading dealers in cosmetics had thousands of kinds on their shelves. Scores of new makers came every week to solicit them. No line dominated. When a woman became converted to one product, and went to a store to get it, she faced a dozen demonstrators who tried to sell other lines.

I sent men to Paris and Vienna to secure something unique, some claims to give me an advantage. But they found none. So I decided to abandon this line.

Just at that time Edna Wallace Hopper played an engagement in Chicago. One morning Mandel Brothers announced in the papers that she would appear in person that afternoon in their beauty department on the fourth floor. I sent an emissary there, and she found the floor crowded. Every other department on the floor had to yield its space to accommodate the women who flocked to see Miss Hopper.

Edna Wallace Hopper had attained a grandmother's age. Many of the older women had seen her in her prime, back in the early 'nineties. She met them looking like a girl of nineteen, with hair, figure, and complexion like a debutante's. Every woman, of course, was anxious to learn the secrets of her youth and beauty.

The manager of Mandels advised her to call on me. He said: "You should capitalize that fame of yours. You should teach other women to do what you have done."

The next day Edna Wallace Hopper called on me. She brought with her countless articles which had been published about her. Also many pages she had written herself on this subject of youth extension.

That day I found my theory. Here was a woman, the most talked-about woman in America. A woman who had made herself a famous beauty thirty-five years ago. A woman who had kept that beauty to a grand old age. And all through beauty helps she had searched the whole world to discover.

I made a contract with her. She was to give me her formulas, her name, and prestige. I was to prepare those products for other women, exactly as she used them. She had spent fortunes to secure those formulas. She was the most prominent example living of what beauty helps could do. On those lines we have founded a large cosmetic business.

We have never had a salesman. We have never asked a dealer to buy. We have confined our efforts to the consumer. We have tried to win women's respect for the research Miss Hopper has conducted. Then we have let those women induce dealers to supply them.

A great many makers, starting out, try to sell their products two and three times over. They try to sell the wholesaler, and the wholesaler today wants some 20 per cent. He can do nothing for us save to fill the orders that we bring. He quotes his business expense, largely made up of efforts to get business from his competitors. He wants us to pay our share, though it matters not in the slightest to us from whom a dealer buys. His salesmen can do nothing for us.

The retailer tries to profit to the utmost from every new adventurer. Send a salesman to him, and he is bound to demand some advantage. He wants a dozen free in ten, or some such extra profit.

Any such concession is a handicap, hard to overcome. Your whole success depends on the consumer. If the consumer is induced to demand what you offer, the dealer will obtain it. If the dealer wants it, the wholesaler will supply it.

Many of the wrecks in advertising come from trying to sell things over and over. One first sells to the jobber, and he demands a large percentage. Then he tries to sell to the retailer. He wants free goods and extra margins. Yet all the results depend on the consumer. All your wholesale demand, all your retail demand, depends on your influence with the consumer.

Never forget that. Jobbers and retailers have their own brands. What trade they can influence is never directed toward products you control. They are not trying to give you a whip-hold. If they can influence sales, they make four times as much on products of their own.

In that fact lies one of the most pitiful phases in advertising adventures. The advertiser spends his money to convert consumers. Then he pays salesmen to sell his goods to jobbers and to retailers. He gives concessions and inducements, just to get them to supply the demand he creates. As a result, there is little left for him. And he must pay all the expenses.

One can never win out in that way. It is like a man who tries to do business with excessive overhead. He bears the expense, the risk, and the effort, and his profits are dissipated.

Today the Edna Wallace Hopper line embraces twenty-three products. Each is a formula Miss Hopper has discovered. When a woman tries one of them she desires to try the rest. The converts to Miss Hopper are converts to her line. So our average in this line is $1.78 per sale. That as compared with 50 cents for a tooth paste, 35 cents for a shaving cream, 10 cents for a soap, etc. Our profit on what we sell from our advertising would never pay the cost. But one thing sells another. That is so in many lines. The whole profit comes in auxiliaries.

This is one of many enterprises I have started in this new régime. Some will fail, but the failures will cost us a trifle. Had I failed for the other fellow they would have cost just as much. The successes will win millions.

So that is my future. Instead of confining myself to building businesses for others on a temporary commission, I have started for myself the enterprises which seem to promise profit. If even one turns out as scores have turned out under my direction, it will win me more than I ever won from writing.

But this is not, as I well realize, good advice to the majority. The average man should work under direction. Success depends on many qualities, of which he has but few. My present adventure is made after decades of working in cooperation.

Let those who can deduce from this experience suggestion and direction. I have tried to point out the only ways to success in advertising. Those ways lead in many directions. Let each one decide what is best.

Chapter Nineteen

Some things personal

As this is a record of success in my particular line of endeavor, and an urge to others, it may be well to set down something about my private life, my idiosyncrasies, habits, and desires as these are related to what I have gained by success.

I have always been an addict to work. I love work as other men love play. It is both my occupation and my recreation. As a boy, the necessity for self-support after school hours kept me from the playgrounds. As a man, my desire to learn all that I could about salesmanship has kept me from wasting time. The only game I ever learned is business. To me it has been all-absorbing. I have never played baseball, golf, or tennis. My mother's Scotch Presbyterianism prohibited dancing, cards, and theaters, and I have never in later years learned to enjoy them. I have owned automobiles since their earliest introduction, but I rarely drive myself.

My chief philanthropy has been teaching boys and men to love work. I have long been interested in an association which takes delinquent boys from the juvenile courts and puts them to work on a farm. It has saved many hundreds of boys in that way. In going to Chicago from my country home I arrive at six o'clock in the morning. For years I went immediately to Grant Park where scores of tramps were sleeping on newspapers, and I spent an hour or more in trying to interest them in work. I am a director of the Volunteers of America, and my particular interest is in prison work. I have accompanied Maud Ballington Booth in her lectures in Joliet prison. I have helped to support Hope House in Chicago, a temporary home for the prisoners we get out on parole. My principal contribution to that effort has been a Sunday afternoon lecture on "The Joy of Work."

I have written magazine articles to argue that both boys and girls should work. I have ever insisted that my unmarried sister keep at work as I do, for the sake of her happiness. She is still teaching in the high schools of Grand Rapids. I sent one of my daughters to work on the stage. The other one married soon after graduation from Smith College. She went to work as a mother, then as president of women's clubs—two at one time. Then to some extent as a lecturer. My wife works some fourteen hours a day. She is our chief gardener, and as such has developed the finest flower gardens in Michigan. Hundreds of people from near and far come to view them every summer. She manages a large country home which is always filled with guests. We figure that we serve here 3,500 breakfasts in a summer season. She is also a musician, devoting to her practice some six hours a day. In Chicago she is famous as a charity worker.

When we had unmarried daughters our house was filled with young men on vacation. I let them know that I did not approve of their idleness. My arguments sent many of them to work in their college vacations, acquiring habits to aid their careers, and I have the satisfaction of knowing that in that way I helped many of them to success. They found that pocketing orders was more fun than pocketing balls. That winning a contract was better than winning a trophy.

My confinement to business has not been due to any love of money or fame. I have not even had a conscious desire to succeed. Money means nothing to me, save that my Scotch instinct rebels at waste. I do not even want to leave it to my children. They already have what is good for them. I want their husbands to have the joy that I had, of making their own success, so I do not deprive them of any incentive.

I long lived in utter poverty where hunger and I were pals. When I entered business I had to miss two meals a week to pay my laundry bills. I have also lived in luxury, spending as high as $140,000 a year. It has made little difference to me. I was as happy in one condition as the other. I do not think we can go back to humble conditions without pangs, but I am sure that men can be as happy on one plateau as another.

The happiest man I know is a neighbor of mine who never made more than $125 per month. Out of that he saved enough to build six small houses which he rents. Then he retired on the income. He spends his summers on my lake, working in his gardens; his winters in Florida. I often go down to his cottage for a lesson in content.

Until the income tax was established I kept no record of my earnings. Their volume meant nothing to me. Their ups and downs did not affect me in the least. My wife collects all my revenues and pays all the bills. I never sign a check. I have not the slightest idea of the money invested in my country place or the cost of any item. Knowing these costs would make me unhappy, because of something mother bred in me. But the general realization that these things cost much money does not affect me at all.

In my personal expenses I am very economical. I have always dressed rather shabbily. Until my wife rebelled I wore ready-made clothes. Now I dodge expensive tailors. At the present writing I have not had a new suit in two years. My limit on shoes is $6.50. When I go to a hotel I order in a modest way.

This is all recited to indicate that my incentive for work was not money. Nor was it fame or position. I care nothing for either out here in the woods among simple people where I have built my home. All things are handicaps which in any way seem to place me above my fellows. Here in the country we all meet on equality.

I have worked for the fun of working and because work became a habit with me. Then later in business because I realized that somebody had to do a deal of hard work to get advertising out of its swaddling clothes.

Lord & Thomas first offered me a position when I was twenty-five, living in Grand Rapids. I went to Chicago to discuss the opportunity with the founders of the business. The agency had no copywriters then. It was largely a brokerage business, bidding against other agencies on a fixed amount of space. The advertisers prepared their own ads. and sent electrotypes. The profitable part of the business was in developing schemes to get advertisers to spend money. The proposition was made to me because I had proved myself a scheme man in the Bissell Carpet Sweeper Company. There was no thought of profit to the advertiser.

I was young and inexperienced, but I had sense enough to realize that such ideas of advertising could not go far. My training had already taught me the necessity for traceable results. So I declined the proposition of Lord & Thomas, with its 60 per cent increase in salary, and continued my struggles to sell products at a profit. It was sixteen years thereafter when Lord & Thomas, under different auspices, again invited me to join them.

What have I gained by these many years of exceptional application? I have gained what others gain by medical research, by spending their lives in a laboratory. My life work has been research in advertising. Now I have the privilege of setting down my findings for the men who follow me. I have the hope that the record will save to many the mistakes of the pioneers and the years that I spent to correct them. I have gained what Thomas A. Edison has gained by his twenty hours a day— the satisfaction of knowing that I have discovered some enduring principles.

Many argue that advertising is changing, that the times call for something new. Certainly the tempo of life in America is changing. Fads, fancies, and desires change like a kaleidoscope. Certain styles in advertising are changing. It is and always has been necessary to give to every campaign a different key-note. Imitators never succeed. But human nature does not change. The principles set down in this book are as enduring as the Alps.

Advertising is far more difficult than it used to be because the cost is higher and there is so much able competition. But every new difficulty increases the necessity for scientific advertising.

As I write this I look down a beautiful lake to which I first came as a boy of six. At the end is a village, once a lumbering town, where my grandfather was the Baptist minister. Within my view are the hills which I plowed as a boy, still clothed with the vineyards which I picked. Here my uncle had a fruit farm which became my home. Here I worked every summer and some winters until I went into business. Here reside still some of my boyhood playmates.

Down there is a point which used to have a dock. From that dock I used to load as high as 1,800 baskets of peaches in a day. From that dock I took the boat one night at the age of eighteen, tears streaming down my cheeks, to enter the world of business. Many hard years went by before I saw this boyhood home again.

Then the homing instinct brought me back. I bought a bluff of virgin forest which I had always loved as a boy, and named it Pineycrest. There I built my home which for seventeen years I have enlarged and developed into a paradise. A half-mile of flower gardens extend into the lake. The lawns are always alive with delightful friends, relatives, and grandchildren.

Here I do what I love to do in beautiful surroundings. Here a mile apart are the contrasts to show what I have gained by my efforts. Here remain some who never dared, to show me what might have been. Here is my motherland, here my tabernacle, here my home.

I am sure that no man has gained more from life than I have—more of true happiness and content. I trace that to the love of simple things, of common people, which made my success in advertising.

Here at our week-end parties I meet many successful men in a most intimate way. I envy none of them. The happiest are those who live closest to nature, an essential to advertising success. So I conclude that this vocation, depending as it does on love and knowledge of the masses, offers many rewards beyond money.

THE END

CLAUDE C. HOPKINS

Scientific
advertising

CHAPTER ONE

How advertising laws
are established

The time has come when advertising has in some hands reached the status of a science. It is based on fixed principles and is reasonably exact. The causes and effects have been analyzed until they are well understood. The correct methods of procedure have been proved and established. We know what is most effective, and we act on basic laws.

Advertising, once a gamble, has thus become, under able direction, one of the safest of business ventures. Certainly no other enterprise with comparable possibilities need involve so little risk.

Therefore this book deals, not with theories and opinions, but with well-proved principles and facts. It is written as a text book for students and a safe guide for advertisers. Every statement has been weighed. The book is confined to established fundamentals. If we enter any realms of uncertainty we shall carefully denote them.

The present status of advertising is due to many reasons. Much national advertising has long been handled by large organizations known as advertising agencies. Some of these agencies, in their hundreds of campaigns, have tested and compared thousands of plans and ideas. The results have been watched and recorded, so no lessons have been lost.

Such agencies employ a high grade of talent. None but able and experienced men can meet the requirements in national advertising. Working in co-operation, learning from each other and from each new undertaking, some of these men develop into masters.

Individuals may come and go, but they leave their records and ideas behind them. These become a part of the organization's equipment, and a guide to all who follow. Thus, in the course of decades, such agencies become storehouses of advertising experiences, proved principles, and methods.

The larger agencies also come into intimate contact with experts in every department of business. Their clients are usually dominating concerns. So they see the results of countless methods and policies. They become a clearing house for everything pertaining to merchandising. Nearly every selling question which arises in business is accurately answered by many experiences.

Under these conditions, where they long exist, advertising and merchandising become exact sciences. Every course is charted. The compass of accurate knowledge directs the shortest, safest, cheapest course to any destination.

We learn the principles and prove them by repeated tests. This is done through keyed advertising, by traced returns, largely by the use of coupons. We compare one way with many others, backward and forward, and record the results. When one method invariably proves best, that method becomes a fixed principle.

Mail order advertising is traced down to the fraction of a penny. The cost per reply and cost per dollar of sale show up with utter exactness.

One ad is compared with another, one method with another. Headlines, settings, sizes, arguments and pictures are compared. To reduce the cost of results even one per cent means much in some mail order advertising. So no guesswork is permitted. One must know what is best. Thus mail order advertising first established many of our basic laws.

In lines where direct returns are impossible we compare one town with another. Scores of methods may be compared in this way, measured by cost of sales.

But the most common way is by use of the coupon. We offer a sample, a book, a free package or something to induce direct replies. Thus we learn the amount of action which each ad engenders.

But those figures are not final. One ad may bring too many worthless replies, another replies that are valuable. So our final conclusions are always based on cost per customer or cost per dollar of sale.

These coupon plans are dealt with further in the chapter on "Test Campaigns." Here we explain only how we employ them to discover advertising principles.

In a large agency coupon returns are watched and recorded on hundreds of different lines. In a single line they are sometimes recorded on thousands of separate ads. Thus we test everything pertaining to advertising. We answer nearly every possible question by multitudinous traced returns.

Some things we learn in this way apply only to particular lines. But even those supply basic principles for analogous undertakings.

Others apply to all lines. They become fundamentals for advertising in general. They are universally applied. No wise advertiser will ever depart from those unvarying laws.

We propose in this book to deal with those fundamentals, those universal principles. To teach only established technic. There is that technic in advertising, as in all art, science and mechanics. And it is, as in all lines, a basic essential.

The lack of those fundamentals has been the main trouble with advertising of the past. Each worker was a law to himself. All previous knowledge, all progress in the line, was a closed book to him. It was like a man trying to build a modern locomotive without first ascertaining what others had done. It was like a Columbus starting out to find an undiscovered land.

Men were guided by whims and fancies—vagrant, changing breezes. They rarely arrived at their port. When they did—by accident—it was by a long roundabout course.

Each early mariner in this sea mapped his own separate course. There were no charts to guide him. Not a lighthouse marked a harbor, not a buoy showed a reef. The wrecks were unrecorded, so countless ventures came to grief on the same rocks and shoals.

Advertising was then a gamble—a speculation of the rashest sort. One man's guess on the proper course was as likely to be as good as another's. There were no safe pilots, because few sailed the same course twice.

That condition has been corrected. Now the only uncertainties pertain to people and to products, not to methods. It is hard to measure human idiosyncrasies, the preferences and prejudices, the likes and dislikes that exist. We cannot say that an article will be popular, but we know how to find out very quickly. We do know how to sell it in the most effective way.

Ventures may fail, but the failures are not disasters. Losses, when they occur, are but trifling.

And the causes are factors which have nothing to do with the advertising.

Advertising has flourished under these new conditions. It has multiplied in volume, in prestige and respect. The perils have been almost eliminated. The results have increased many fold. Just because the gamble has become a science, the speculation a very conservative business.

These facts should be recognized by all. This is no proper field for sophistry or theory, or for any other will-o'-the-wisp. The blind leading the blind is ridiculous. It is pitiful in a field with such vast possibilities. Success is a rarity, maximum success an impossibility, unless one is guided by laws as immutable as the law of gravitation.

So our main purpose here is to set down those laws, and to tell you how to prove them for yourself. After them come a myriad variations. No two advertising campaigns are ever conducted on lines that are identical. Individuality is an essential. Imitation is a reproach. But those variable things which depend on ingenuity have no place in a text book on advertising. This is for groundwork only.

Our hope is to foster advertising through a better understanding. To place it on a business basis. To have it recognized as among the safest, surest ventures which lead to large returns.

Thousands of conspicuous successes show its possibilities. Their variety points out its almost unlimited scope. Yet thousands who need it—who can never attain their deserts without it—still look upon its accomplishments as somewhat accidental.

That was so, but it is not so now. We hope that this book will throw some new lights on the subject.

CHAPTER TWO

Just
salesmanship

To properly understand advertising or to learn even its rudiments one must start with the right conception. Advertising is salesmanship. Its principles are the principles of salesmanship. Successes and failures in both lines are due to like causes. Thus every advertising question should be answered by the salesman's standards.

Let us emphasize that point. The only purpose of advertising is to make sales. It is profitable or unprofitable according to its actual sales.

It is not for general effect. It is not to keep your name before the people. It is not primarily to aid your other salesmen.

Treat it as a salesman. Force it to justify itself. Compare it with other salesmen. Figure its cost and result. Accept no excuses which good salesmen do not make. Then you will not go far wrong.

The difference is only in degree. Advertising is multiplied salesmanship. It may appeal to thousands while the salesman talks to one. It involves a corresponding cost. Some people spend $10 per word on an average advertisement. Therefore every ad should be a super-salesman.

A salesman's mistake may cost little. An advertising mistake may cost a thousand times as much. Be more cautious, more exacting, therefore.

A mediocre salesman may affect a small part of your trade. Mediocre advertising affects all of your trade.

Many think of advertising as ad-writing. Literary qualifications have no more to do with it than oratory has with salesmanship.

One must be able to express himself briefly, clearly and convincingly, just as a salesman must. But fine writing is a distinct disadvantage. So is unique literary style. They take attention from the subject. They reveal the hook. Any studied attempt to sell, if apparent, creates corresponding resistance.

That is so in personal salesmanship as in salesmanship-in-print. Fine talkers are rarely good salesmen. They inspire buyers with the fear of over-influence. They create the suspicion that an effort is made to sell them on other lines than merit.

Successful salesmen are rarely good speech makers. They have few oratorical graces. They are plain and sincere men who know their customers and know their lines. So it is in ad-writing.

Many of the ablest men in advertising are graduate salesmen. The best we know have been house-to-house canvassers. They may know little of grammar, nothing of rhetoric, but they know how to use words that convince.

There is one simple and right way to answer many advertising questions. Ask yourself, "Would this help a salesman sell the goods?" "Would it help me sell them if I met the buyer in person?"

A fair answer to those questions avoids countless mistakes. But when one tries to show off, or does things merely to please himself, he is little likely to strike a chord which leads people to spend money.

Some argue for slogans, some like clever conceits. Would you use them in personal salesmanship? Can you imagine a customer whom such things would impress? If not, don't rely on them for selling in print.

Some say, "Be very brief. People will read but little." Would you say that to a salesman? With a prospect standing before him, would you confine him to any certain number of words? That would be an unthinkable handicap.

So in advertising. The only readers we get are people whom our subject interests. No one reads ads for amusement, long or short. Consider them as prospects standing before you, seeking for information. Give them enough to get action.

Some advocate large type and big headlines. Yet they do not admire salesmen who talk in loud voices. People read all they care to read in 8-point type. Our magazines and newspapers are printed in that type. Folks are accustomed to it. Anything larger is like loud conversation. It gains no attention worth while. It may not be offensive, but it is useless and wasteful. It multiplies the cost of your story. And to many it seems loud and blatant.

Others look for something queer and unusual. They want ads distinctive in style or illustration. Would you want that in a salesman? Do not men who act and dress in normal ways make a far better impression?

Some insist on dressy ads. That is all right to a certain degree, but it is quite unimportant. Some poorly-dressed ads, like poorly-dressed men, prove to be excellent salesmen. Over-dress in either is a fault.

So with countless questions. Measure them by salesmen's standards, not by amusement standards. Ads are not written to entertain. When they do, those entertainment seekers are little likely to be the people whom you want.

That is one of the greatest advertising faults. Ad-writers abandon their parts. They forget they are salesmen and try to be performers. Instead of sales, they seek applause.

When you plan and prepare an advertisement, keep before you a typical buyer. Your subject, your headline has gained his or her attention. Then in everything be guided by what you would do if you met the buyer face-to-face. If you are a normal man and a good salesman you will then do your level best.

Don't think of people in the mass. That gives you a blurred view. Think of a typical individual, man or woman, who is likely to want what you sell. Don't try to be amusing. Money spending is a serious matter. Don't boast, for all people resent it. Don't try to show off. Do just what you think a good salesman should do with a half-sold person before him.

Some advertising men go out in person and sell to people before they plan or write an ad. One of the ablest of them has spent weeks on one article, selling from house to house. In this way they learn the reactions from different forms of argument and approach. They learn what possible buyers want and the factors which don't appeal. It is quite customary to interview hundreds of possible customers.

Others send out questionnaires to learn the attitude of buyers. In some way all must learn how to strike responsive chords. Guesswork is very expensive.

The maker of an advertised article knows the manufacturing side and probably the dealer's side. But this very knowledge often leads him astray in respect to consumers. His interests are not their interests.

The advertising man studies the consumer. He tries to place himself in the position of the buyer. His success largely depends on doing that to the exclusion of everything else.

This book will contain no more important chapter than this one on salesmanship. The reason for most of the non-successes in advertising is trying to sell people what they do not want. But next to that comes the lack of true salesmanship.

Ads are planned and written with some utterly wrong conception. They are written to please the seller. The interests of the buyer are forgotten. One can never sell goods profitably, in person or in print, when that attitude exists.

CHAPTER THREE

Offer
service

R emember that the people you address are selfish, as we all are. They care nothing about your interest or your profit. They seek service for themselves. Ignoring this fact is a common mistake and a costly mistake in advertising. Ads say in effect, "Buy my brand. Give me the trade you give to others. Let me have the money." That is not a popular appeal.

The best ads ask no one to buy. That is useless. Often they do not quote a price. They do not say that dealers handle the product.

The ads are based entirely on service. They offer wanted information. They cite advantages to users. Perhaps they offer a sample, or to buy the first package, or to send something on approval, so the customer may prove the claims without any cost or risk.

Some of these ads seem altruistic. But they are based on a knowledge of human nature. The writers know how people are led to buy.

Here again is salesmanship. The good salesman does not merely cry a name. He doesn't say, "Buy my article." He pictures the customer's side of his service until the natural result is to buy.

A brush maker has some 2,000 canvassers who sell brushes from house to house. He is enormously successful in a line which would seem very difficult. And it would be if his men asked the housewives to buy.

But they don't. They go to the door and say, "I was sent here to give you a brush. I have samples here and I want you to take your choice."

The housewife is all smiles and attention. In picking out one brush she sees several she wants. She is also anxious to reciprocate the gift. So the salesman gets an order.

Another concern sells coffee, etc., by wagons in some 500 cities. The man drops in with a half-pound of coffee and says, "Accept this package and try it. I'll come back in a few days to ask how you like it."

Even when he comes back he doesn't ask for an order. He explains that he wants to send the woman a fine kitchen utensil. It isn't free, but if she likes the coffee he will credit five cents on each pound she buys until she has paid for the article. Always some service.

The maker of an electric sewing machine motor found advertising difficult. So, on good advice, he ceased soliciting a purchase. He offered to send to any home, through any dealer, a motor for one week's use. With it would come a man to show how to operate. "Let us help you for a week without cost or obligation," said the ad. Such an offer was resistless, and about nine in ten of the trials led to sales.

So in many, many lines. Cigar makers send out boxes to anyone and say, "Smoke ten, then keep them or return them, as you wish."

Makers of books, typewriters, washing machines, kitchen cabinets, vacuum sweepers, etc., send out their products without any prepayment. They say, "Use them a week, then do as you wish." Practically all merchandise sold by mail is sent subject to return.

These are all common principles of salesmanship. The most ignorant peddler applies them. Yet the salesman-in-print very often forgets them. He talks about his interests. He blazons a name, as though that was of any importance. His phrase is, "Drive people to the stores," and that is his attitude in everything he says.

People can be coaxed but not driven. Whatever they do they do to please themselves. Many fewer mistakes would be made in advertising if these facts were never forgotten.

CHAPTER FOUR

Mail order
advertising—what it teaches

The severest test of an advertising man is in
selling goods by mail. But that is a school
from which he must graduate before he can hope
for success. There cost and result are immediately
apparent. False theories melt away like snowflakes
in the sun. The advertising is profitable or it is not,
clearly on the face of returns. Figures which do
not lie tell one at once the merits of an ad.

This puts men on their mettle. All guesswork is
eliminated. Every mistake is conspicuous. One
quickly loses his conceit by learning how often his
judgment errs—often nine times in ten.

There one learns that advertising must be done
on a scientific basis to have any fair chance at success. And he learns how every wasted dollar adds
to the cost of results.

Here he is taught efficiency and economy under a master who can't be fooled. Then, and then only, is he apt to apply the same principles and keys to all advertising.

A man was selling a five-dollar article. The replies from his ad cost him 85 cents. Another man submitted an ad which he thought better. The replies cost $14.20 each. Another man submitted an ad which for two years brought replies at an average of 41 cents each.

Consider that difference, on 250,000 replies per year. Think how valuable was the man who cut the cost in two. Think what it would have meant to have continued that $14.20 ad without any key on returns.

Yet there are thousands of advertisers who do just that. They spend large sums on a guess. And they are doing what that man did—paying for sales from 2 to 35 times what they need cost.

A study of mail order advertising reveals many things worth learning. It is a prime subject for study. In the first place, if continued, you know that it pays. It is therefore good advertising as applied to that line.

The probability is that the ad has resulted from many traced comparisons. It is therefore the best advertising yet discovered for that line.

Study those ads with respect. There is proved advertising, not theoretical. It will not deceive you. The lessons it teaches are principles which wise men apply to all advertising.

Mail order advertising is always set in small type. It is usually set in smaller type than ordinary print. That economy of space is universal. So it proves conclusively that larger type does not pay.

Remember that when you double your space by doubling the size of your type. The ad may still be profitable. But traced returns have proved that you are paying a double price for sales.

In mail order advertising there is no waste of space. Every line is utilized. Borders are rarely used. Remember that when you are tempted to leave valuable space unoccupied.

In mail order advertising there is no palaver. There is no boasting, save of super-service. There is no useless talk. There is no attempt at entertainment. There is nothing to amuse.

Mail order advertising usually contains a coupon. That is there to get some action from the converts partly made. It is there to cut out as a reminder of something the reader has decided to do.

Mail order advertisers know that readers forget. They are reading a magazine of interest. They may be absorbed in a story. A large percentage of people who read an ad and decide to act will forget that decision in five minutes. The mail order advertiser knows that waste by tests, and he does not propose to accept it. So he inserts that reminder to be cut out, and it turns up when the reader is ready to act.

In mail order advertising the pictures are always to the point. They are salesmen in themselves. They earn the space they occupy. The size is gauged by their importance. The picture of a dress one is trying to sell may occupy much space. Less important things get smaller spaces.

Pictures in ordinary advertising may teach little. They probably result from whims. But pictures in mail order advertising may form half the cost of selling. And you may be sure that everything about them has been decided by many comparative tests.

Before you use useless pictures, merely to decorate or interest, look over some mail order ads. Mark what their verdict is.

A man advertised an incubator to be sold by mail. Type ads with right headlines brought excellent returns. But he conceived the idea that a striking picture would increase those returns. So he increased his space 50 per cent to add a row of chickens in silhouette.

It did make a striking ad, but his cost per reply was increased by exactly that 50 per cent. The new ad, costing one-half more for every insertion, brought not one added sale.

The man learned that incubator buyers were practical people. They were looking for attractive offers, not for pictures.

Think of the countless untraced campaigns where a whim of that kind costs half the advertising money without a penny of return. And it may go on year after year.

Mail order advertising tells a complete story if the purpose is to make an immediate sale. You see no limitations there on amount of copy.

The motto there is, "The more you tell the more you sell." And it has never failed to prove out so in any test we know.

Sometimes the advertiser uses small ads, sometimes large ads. None are too small to tell a reasonable story. But an ad twice larger brings twice the returns. A four-times-larger ad brings four times the returns, and usually some in addition.

But this occurs only when the larger space is utilized as well as the small space. Set half-page copy in a page space and you double the cost of returns. We have seen many a test prove that.

Look at an ad of the Mead Cycle Company—a typical mail order ad. These have been running for many years. The ads are unchanging. Mr. Mead told the writer that not for $10,000 would he change a single word in his ads.

For many years he compared one ad with another. And the ads you see today are the final result of all those experiments. Note the picture he uses, the headlines, the economy of space, the small type. Those ads are as near perfect for their purpose as an ad can be.

So with any other mail order ad which has long continued. Every feature, every word and picture teaches advertising at its best. You may not like them. You may say they are unattractive, crowded, hard to read—anything you will. But the test of results has proved those ads the best salesmen those lines have yet discovered. And they certainly pay.

Mail order advertising is the court of last resort. You may get the same instruction, if you will, by keying other ads. But mail order ads are models. They are selling goods profitably in a difficult way. It is far harder to get mail orders than to send buyers to the stores. It is hard to sell goods which can't be seen. Ads which do that are excellent examples of what advertising should be.

We cannot often follow all the principles of mail order advertising, though we know we should. The advertiser forces a compromise. Perhaps pride in our ads has an influence. But every departure from those principles adds to our selling cost. Therefore it is always a question of what we are willing to pay for our frivolities.

We can at least know what we pay. We can make keyed comparisons, one ad with another. Whenever we do we invariably find that the nearer we get to proved mail order copy the more customers we get for our money.

This is another important chapter. Think it over. What real difference is there between inducing a customer to order by mail or order from his dealer? Why should the methods of salesmanship differ?

They should not. When they do, it is for one of two reasons. Either the advertiser does not know what the mail order advertiser knows. He is advertising blindly. Or he is deliberately sacrificing a percentage of his returns to gratify some desire.

There is some apology for that, just as there is for fine offices and buildings. Most of us can afford to do something for pride and opinion. But let us know what we are doing. Let us know the cost of our pride. Then, if our advertising fails to bring the wanted returns, let us go back to our model— a good mail order ad—and eliminate some of our waste.

CHAPTER FIVE

Headlines

The difference between advertising and personal salesmanship lies largely in personal contact. The salesman is there to demand attention. He cannot well be ignored. The advertisement can be ignored.

But the salesman wastes much of his time on prospects whom he never can hope to interest. He cannot pick them out. The advertisement is read only by interested people who, by their own volition, study what we have to say.

The purpose of a headline is to pick out people you can interest. You wish to talk to someone in a crowd. So the first thing you say is, "Hey there, Bill Jones" to get the right person's attention.

So in an advertisement. What you have will interest certain people only, and for certain reasons.

You care only for those people. Then create a headline which will hail those people only.

Perhaps a blind headline or some clever conceit will attract many times as many. But they may consist mostly of impossible subjects for what you have to offer. And the people you are after may never realize that the ad refers to something they may want.

Headlines on ads are like headlines on news items. Nobody reads a whole newspaper. One is interested in financial news, one in political, one in society, one in cookery, one in sports, etc. There are whole pages in any newspaper which we never scan at all. Yet other people may turn directly to those pages.

We pick out what we wish to read by headlines, and we don't want those headlines misleading. The writing of headlines is one of the greatest journalistic arts. They either conceal or reveal an interest.

Suppose a newspaper article stated that a certain woman was the most beautiful in the city. That article would be of intense interest to that woman and her friends. But neither she nor her friends would ever read it if the headline was "Egyptian Psychology."

So in advertising. It is commonly said that people do not read advertisements. That is silly, of course. We who spend millions in advertising and watch the returns marvel at the readers we get.

Again and again we see 20 per cent of all the readers of a newspaper cut out a certain coupon.

But people do not read ads for amusement. They don't read ads which, at a glance, seem to offer nothing interesting. A double-page ad on women's dresses will not gain a glance from a man. Nor will a shaving cream ad from a woman.

Always bear these facts in mind. People are hurried. The average person worth cultivating has too much to read. They skip three-fourths of the reading matter which they pay to get. They are not going to read your business talk unless you make it worth their while and let the headline show it.

People will not be bored in print. They may listen politely at a dinner table to boasts and personalities, life histories, etc. But in print they choose their own companions, their own subjects. They want to be amused or benefited. They want economy, beauty, labor saving, good things to eat and wear. There may be products which interest them more than anything else in a magazine. But they will never know it unless the headline or the picture tells them.

The writer of this chapter spends far more time on headlines than on writing. He often spends hours on a single headline. Often scores of headlines are discarded before the right one is selected. For the entire return from an ad depends on attracting the right sort of readers. The best of salesmanship has no chance whatever unless we get a hearing.

The vast difference in headlines is shown by keyed returns which this book advocates. The identical ad run with various headlines differs tremendously in its returns. It is not uncommon for a change in headlines to multiply returns from five to ten times over.

So we compare headlines until we know what sort of appeal pays best. That differs in every line, of course.

The writer has before him keyed returns on nearly two thousand headlines used on a single product. The story in these ads is nearly identical. But the returns vary enormously, due to the headlines. So with every keyed return in our record appears the headline that we used.

Thus we learn what type of headline has the most wide-spread appeal. The product has many uses. It fosters beauty. It prevents disease. It aids daintiness and cleanliness. We learn to exactness which quality most of our readers seek.

That does not mean that we neglect the others. One sort of appeal may bring half the returns of another, yet be important enough to be profitable. We overlook no field that pays. But we know what proportion of our ads should, in the headline, attract any certain class.

For this same reason we employ a vast variety of ads. If we are using twenty magazines we may use twenty separate ads. This because circulations overlap, and because a considerable percentage of people are attracted by each of several forms of approach. We wish to reach them all.

On a soap, for instance, the headline "Keep Clean" might attract a very small percentage. It is too commonplace. So might the headline, "No animal fats." People may not care much about that. The headline, "It floats" might prove interesting. But a headline referring to beauty or complexion might attract many times as many.

An automobile ad might refer in the headline to a good universal joint. It might fall flat, because so few buyers think of universal joints. The same ad with a headline, "The Sportiest of Sport Bodies," might outpull the other by fifty to one.

This is enough to suggest the importance of headlines. Anyone who keys ads will be amazed at the difference. The appeals we like best will rarely prove best, because we do not know enough people to average up their desires. So we learn on each line by experiment.

But back of all lie fixed principles. You are presenting an ad to millions. Among them is a percentage, small or large, whom you hope to interest. Go after that percentage and try to strike the chord that responds. If you are advertising corsets, men and children don't interest you. If you are advertising cigars, you have no use for non-smokers. Razors won't attract women, rouge will not interest men.

Don't think that those millions will read your ads to find out if your product interests. They will decide by a glance—by your headline or your pictures. Address the people you seek, and them only.

Psychology

The competent advertising man must understand psychology. The more he knows about it the better. He must learn that certain effects lead to certain reactions, and use that knowledge to increase results and avoid mistakes.

Human nature is perpetual. In most respects it is the same today as in the time of Caesar. So the principles of psychology are fixed and enduring. You will never need to unlearn what you learn about them.

We learn, for instance, that curiosity is one of the strongest of human incentives. We employ it whenever we can. Puffed Wheat and Puffed Rice were made successful largely through curiosity. "Grains puffed to 8 times normal size." "Foods shot from guns." "125 million steam explosions caused in every kernel." These foods were failures before that factor was discovered.

We learn that cheapness is not a strong appeal. Americans are extravagant. They want bargains but not cheapness. They want to feel that they can afford to eat and have and wear the best. Treat them as though they could not and they resent your attitude.

We learn that people judge largely by price. They are not experts. In the British National Gallery is a painting which is announced in the catalog to have cost $750,000. Most people at first pass it by at a glance. Then later they get farther on in the catalog and learn what the painting cost. They return then and surround it.

A department store advertised at one Easter time a $1,000 hat, and the floor could not hold the women who came to see it.

We often employ this factor in psychology. Perhaps we are advertising a valuable formula. To merely say that would not be impressive. So we state—as a fact—that we paid $100,000 for that formula. That statement when tried has won a wealth of respect.

Many articles are sold under guarantee—so commonly sold that guarantees have ceased to be impressive. But one concern made a fortune by offering a dealer's signed warrant. The dealer to whom one paid his money agreed in writing to pay it back if asked. Instead of a far-away stranger, a neighbor gave the warrant. The results have led many to try that plan, and it has always proved effective.

Many have advertised, "Try it for a week. If you don't like it we'll return your money." Then someone conceived the idea of sending goods without any money down, and saying, "Pay in a week if you like them." That proved many times as impressive.

One great advertising man stated the difference in this way: "Two men came to me, each offering me a horse. Both made equal claims. They were good horses, kind and gentle. A child could drive them. One man said, 'Try the horse for a week. If my claims are not true, come back for your money.' The other man also said, 'Try the horse for a week.' But he added, 'Come and pay me then.' I naturally bought the second man's horse."

Now countless things—cigars, typewriters, washing machines, books, etc.—are sent out in this way on approval. And we find that people are honest. The losses are very small.

An advertiser offered a set of books to business men. The advertising was unprofitable, so he consulted another expert. The ads were impressive. The offer seemed attractive. "But," said the second man, "let us add one little touch which I have found effective. Let us offer to put the buyer's name in gilt lettering on each book." That was done, and with scarcely another change in the ads they sold some hundreds of thousands of books.

Through some peculiar kink in human psychology that name in gilt gave much added value to the books.

Many send out small gifts, like memorandum books, to customers and prospects. They get very small results. One man sent out a letter to the effect that he had a leather-covered book with the man's name on it. It was waiting for him and would be sent on request. The form of request was enclosed, and it also asked for certain information. That information indicated lines on which the man might be sold.

Nearly all men, it was found, filled out that request and supplied the information. When a man knows that something belongs to him—something with his name on—he will make the effort to get it, even though the thing is a trifle.

In the same way it is found that an offer limited to a certain class of people is far more effective than a general offer. For instance, an offer limited to veterans of the war. Or to members of a lodge or sect. Or to executives. Those who are entitled to any seeming advantage will go a long way not to lose that advantage.

An advertiser suffered much from substitution. He said, "Look out for substitutes," "Be sure you get this brand," etc., with no effect. Those were selfish appeals.

Then he said, "Try our rivals' too"—said it in his headlines. He invited comparisons and showed that he did not fear them. That corrected the situation. Buyers were careful to get the brand so conspicuously superior that its maker could court a trial of the rest.

Two advertisers offered food products nearly identical. Both offered a full-size package as an introduction. But one gave his package free. The other bought the package. A coupon was good at any store for a package, for which the maker paid retail price.

The first advertiser failed and the second succeeded. The first even lost a large part of the trade he had. He cheapened his product by giving a 15-cent package away. It is hard to pay for an article which has once been free. It is like paying railroad fare after traveling on a pass.

The other gained added respect for his article by paying retail price to let the user try it. An article good enough for the maker to buy is good enough for the user to buy. It is vastly different to pay 15 cents to let you try an article than to simply say "It's free."

So with sampling. Hand an unwanted product to a housewife and she pays it slight respect. She is in no mood to see its virtues. But get her to ask for a sample after reading your story, and she is in a very different position. She knows your claims. She is interested in them, else she would not act. And she expects to find the qualities you told.

There is a great deal in mental impression. Submit five articles exactly alike and five people may each choose one of them. But point out in one some qualities to notice and everyone will find them. The five people then will all choose the same article.

If people can be made sick or well by mental impressions, they can be made to favor a certain brand in that way. And that, on some lines, is the only way to win them.

Two concerns, side by side, sold women's clothing on installments. The appeal, of course, was to poor girls who desired to dress better. One treated them like poor girls and made the bare business offer.

The other put a woman in charge—a motherly, dignified, capable woman. They did business in her name. They used her picture. She signed all ads and letters. She wrote to these girls like a friend. She knew herself what it meant to a girl not to be able to dress her best. She had long sought a chance to supply women good clothes and give them all season to pay. Now she was able to do so, with the aid of the men behind her.

There was no comparison in those two appeals. It was not long before this woman's long-established next-door rival had to quit.

The backers of this business sold housefurnishings on installments. Sending out catalogs promiscuously did not pay. Offering long-time credit often seems like a reflection.

But when a married woman bought garments from Mrs. __, and paid as agreed, they wrote to her something like this: "Mrs. __, whom we know, tells us that you are one of her good customers. She has dealt with you, she says, and you do just as you agree. So we have opened with you a credit account on our books, good any time you wish. When you want anything in furnishings, just order it. Pay nothing in advance. We are very glad to send it without any investigation to a person recommended as you are."

That was flattering. Naturally those people, when they wanted some furniture, would order from that house.

There are endless phases to psychology. Some people know them by instinct. Many of them are taught by experience. But we learn most of them from others. When we see a winning method we note it down for use when occasion offers.

These things are very important. An identical offer made in a different way may bring multiplied returns. Somewhere in the mines of business experience we must find the best method somehow.

CHAPTER SEVEN

Being
specific

P latitudes and generalities roll off the human
understanding like water from a duck. They
leave no impression whatever. To say, "Best in the
world," "Lowest prices in existence," etc. are at
best simply claiming the expected. But superlatives
of that sort are usually damaging. They suggest
looseness of expression, a tendency to exaggerate,
a carelessness of truth. They lead readers to discount all the statements that you make.

People recognize a certain license in selling talk
as they do in poetry. A man may say, "Supreme in
quality" without seeming a liar, though one may
know that other brands are equally as good. One
expects a salesman to put his best foot forward, and
excuses some exaggeration born of enthusiasm. But
just for that reason general statements count for

little. And a man inclined to superlatives must expect that his every statement will be taken with some caution.

But a man who makes a specific claim is either telling the truth or a lie. People do not expect an advertiser to lie. They know that he can't lie in the best mediums. The growing respect for advertising has largely come through a growing regard for its truth.

So a definite statement is usually accepted. Actual figures are not generally discounted. Specific facts, when stated, have their full weight and effect.

This is very important to consider in written or personal salesmanship. The weight of an argument may often be multiplied by making it specific. Say that a tungsten lamp gives more light than a carbon and you leave some doubt. Say that it gives three and one-third times the light and people realize that you have made tests and comparisons.

A dealer may say, "Our prices have been reduced" without creating any marked impression. But when he says, "Our prices have been reduced 25 per cent" he gets the full value of his announcement.

A mail order advertiser sold women's clothing to people of the poorer classes. For years he used the slogan, "Lowest prices in America." His rivals all copied that. Then he guaranteed to undersell any other dealer. His rivals did likewise. Soon those claims became common to every advertiser in his line, and they became commonplace.

Then, under able advice, he changed his statement to "Our net profit is 3 per cent." That was a definite statement and it proved very impressive. With their volume of business it was evident that their prices must be minimum. No one could be expected to do business on less than 3 per cent. The next year their business made a sensational increase.

At one time in the automobile business there was a general impression that profits were excessive. One well-advised advertiser came out with the statement, "Our profit is 9 per cent." Then he cited actual costs on the hidden parts of a $1,500 car. They amounted to $735, without including anything one could easily see. This advertiser made a great success along those lines at that time.

Shaving soaps have long been advertised "Abundant lather," "Does not dry on the face," "Acts quickly," etc. One advertiser had as good a chance as another to impress those claims.

Then a new maker came into the field. It was a tremendously difficult field, for every customer had to be taken from someone else. He stated specific facts. He said, "Multiplies itself in lather 250 times." "Softens the beard in one minute." "Maintains its creamy fullness for ten minutes on the face." "The final result of testing and comparing 130 formulas." Perhaps never in advertising has there been a quicker and greater success in an equally difficult field.

Makers of safety razors have long advertised quick shaves. One maker advertised a 78-second shave. That was definite. It indicated actual tests. That man at once made a sensational advance in his sales.

In the old days all beers were advertised as "Pure." The claim made no impression. The bigger the type used, the bigger the folly. After millions had been spent to impress a platitude, one brewer pictured a plate glass room where beer was cooled in filtered air. He pictured a filter of white wood pulp through which every drop was cleared. He told how bottles were washed four times by machinery. How he went down 4,000 feet for pure water. How 1,018 experiments had been made to attain a yeast to give beer that matchless flavor. And how all the yeast was forever made from that adopted mother cell.

All the claims were such as any brewer might have made. They were mere essentials in ordinary brewing. But he was the first to tell the people about them, while others cried merely "pure beer." He made the greatest success that was ever made in beer advertising.

"Used the world over" is a very elastic claim. Then one advertiser said, "Used by the peoples of 52 nations," and many another has followed.

One statement may take as much room as another, yet a definite statement be many times as effective. The difference is vast. If a claim is worth making, make it in the most impressive way.

All these effects must be studied. Salesmanship-in-print is very expensive. Every word you use may cost $10 to insert. A salesman's loose talk matters little. But when you are talking to millions at enormous cost, the weight of your claims is important.

No generality has any weight whatever. It is like saying, "How do you do?" when you have no intention of inquiring about one's health. But specific claims when made in print are taken at their value.

CHAPTER EIGHT

Tell
your full story

Whatever claim you use to gain attention, the advertisement should tell a story reasonably complete. If you watch returns, you will find that certain claims appeal far more than others. But in usual lines a number of claims appeal to a large percentage. Then present those claims in every ad for their effect on that percentage.

Some advertisers, for the sake of brevity, present one claim at a time. Or they write a serial ad, continued in another issue. There is no greater folly. Those serials almost never connect.

When you once get a person's attention, then is the time to accomplish all you ever hope with him. Bring all your good arguments to bear. Cover every phase of your subject. One fact appeals to some, one to another. Omit any one and a certain percentage will lose the fact which might convince.

People are not apt to read successive advertisements on any single line. No more than you read
a news item twice, or a story. In one reading of an
advertisement one decides for or against a proposition. And that operates against a second reading.
So present to the reader, when once you get him,
every important claim you have.

The best advertisers do that. They learn their
appealing claims by tests—by comparing results
from various headlines. Gradually they accumulate
a list of claims important enough to use. All those
claims appear in every ad thereafter.

The advertisements seem monotonous to the men
who read them all. A complete story is always the
same. But one must consider that the average
reader is only once a reader, probably. And what
you fail to tell him in that ad is something he may
never know.

Some advertisers go so far as to never change
their ads. Single mail order ads often run year after
year without diminishing returns. So with some
general ads. They are perfected ads, embodying
in the best way known all that one has to say.
Advertisers do not expect a second reading. Their
constant returns come from getting new readers.

In every ad consider only new customers. People
using your product are not going to read your ads.
They have already read and decided. You might
advertise month after month to present users that
the product they use is poison, and they would

never know it. So never waste one line of your space to say something to present users, unless you can say it in headlines. Bear in mind always that you address an unconverted prospect.

Any reader of your ad is interested, else he would not be a reader. You are dealing with someone willing to listen. Then do your level best. That reader, if you lose him now, may never again be a reader.

You are like a salesman in a busy man's office. He may have tried again and again to get entree. He may never be admitted again. This is his one chance to get action, and he must employ it to the full.

This again brings up the question of brevity. The most common expression you hear about advertising is that people will not read much. Yet a vast amount of the best-paying advertising shows that people do read much. Then they write for a book, perhaps—for added information.

There is no fixed rule on this subject of brevity. One sentence may tell a complete story on a line like chewing gum. It may on an article like Cream of Wheat. But, whether long or short, an advertising story should be reasonably complete.

A certain man desired a personal car. He cared little about the price. He wanted a car to take pride in, else he felt he would never drive it. But, being a good business man, he wanted value for his money.

His inclination was toward a Rolls-Royce. He also considered a Pierce-Arrow, a Locomobile and others. But these famous cars offered no information. Their advertisements were very short. Evidently the makers considered it undignified to argue comparative merits.

The Marmon, on the contrary, told a complete story. He read columns and books about it. So he bought a Marmon, and was never sorry. But he afterwards learned facts about another car at nearly three times the price which would have sold him that car had he known them.

What folly it is to cry a name in a line like that, plus a few brief generalities. A car may be a lifetime investment. It involves an important expenditure. A man interested enough to buy a car will read a volume about it if the volume is interesting.

So with everything. You may be simply trying to change a woman from one breakfast food to another, or one tooth paste, or one soap. She is wedded to what she is using. Perhaps she has used it for years.

You have a hard proposition. If you do not believe it, go to her in person and try to make the change. Not to merely buy a first package to please you, but to adopt your brand. A man who once does that at a woman's door won't argue for brief advertisements. He will never again say, "A sentence will do," or a name or a claim or a boast.

Nor will the man who traces his results. Note that brief ads are never keyed. Note that every traced ad tells a complete story, though it takes columns to tell.

Never be guided in any way by ads which are untraced. Never do anything because some uninformed advertiser considers that something right. Never be led in new paths by the blind. Apply to your advertising ordinary common sense. Take the opinion of nobody, the verdict of nobody, who knows nothing about his returns.

CHAPTER NINE

Art
in advertising

Pictures in advertising are very expensive. Not in the cost of good art work alone, but in the cost of space. From one-third to one-half of an advertising campaign is often staked on the power of the pictures.

Anything expensive must be effective, else it involves much waste. So art in advertising is a study of paramount importance.

Pictures should not be used merely because they are interesting. Or to attract attention. Or to decorate an ad. We have covered these points else-where. Ads are not written to interest, please or amuse. You are not writing to please the *hoi-polloi*. You are writing on a serious subject—the subject of money-spending. And you address a restricted minority.

Use pictures only to attract those who may profit you. Use them only when they form a better selling argument than the same amount of space set in type.

Mail order advertisers, as we have said, have pictures down to a science. Some use large pictures, some use small, some omit pictures entirely. A noticeable fact is that none of them uses expensive art work. Be sure that all these things are done for reasons made apparent by results.

Any other advertiser should apply the same principles. Or, if none exist which apply to his line, he should work out his own by tests. It is certainly unwise to spend large sums on a dubious adventure.

Pictures in many lines form a major factor. Omitting the lines where the article itself should be pictured. In some lines, like Arrow Collars and in clothing advertising, pictures have proved most convincing. Not only in picturing the collar or the clothes, but in picturing men whom others envy, in surroundings which others covet. The pictures subtly suggest that these articles of apparel will aid men to those desired positions.

So with correspondence schools. Theirs is traced advertising. Picturing men in high positions or taking upward steps forms a very convincing argument.

So with beauty articles. Picturing beautiful

women, admired and attractive, is a supreme inducement. But there is a great advantage in including a fascinated man. Women desire beauty largely because of men. Then show them using their beauty, as women do use it, to gain maximum effect.

Advertising pictures should not be eccentric. Don't treat your subject lightly. Don't lessen respect for yourself or your article by any attempt at frivolity. People do not patronize a clown. There are two things about which men should never joke. One is business, one is home.

An eccentric picture may do you serious damage. One may gain attention by wearing a fool's cap. But he would ruin his selling prospects.

Then a picture which is eccentric or unique takes attention from your subject. You cannot afford to do that. Your main appeal lies in your headline. Over-shadow that and you kill it. Don't, to gain general and useless attention, sacrifice the attention that you want.

Don't be like a salesman who wears conspicuous clothes. The small percentage he appeals to are not usually good buyers. The great majority of the sane and thrifty heartily despise him. Be normal in everything you do when you are seeking confidence and conviction.

Generalities cannot well be applied to art. There are seeming exceptions to most statements. Each line must be studied by itself.

But the picture must help sell the goods. It should help more than anything else could do in like space, else use that something else.

Many pictures tell a story better than type can do. In the advertising of Puffed Grains the pictures of the grains were found to be most effective. They awake curiosity. No figure drawings in that case compare in results with these grains.

Other pictures form a total loss. We have cited cases of that kind. The only way to know, as is with most other questions, is by compared results.

There are disputed questions in art work which we will cite without expressing opinions. They seem to be answered both ways, according to the line which is advertised.

Does it pay better to use fine art work or ordinary? Some advertisers pay up to $2,000 per drawing. They figure that the space is expensive. The art cost is small in comparison. So they consider the best worth its cost.

Others argue that few people have art education. The art judges form a percentage too small to consider. They bring out their ideas, and bring them out well, at a fraction of the cost. Mail order advertisers are generally in this class.

The question is one of small moment. Certainly good art pays as well as mediocre. And the cost of preparing ads is very small compared with the cost of insertion.

Should every ad have a new picture? Or may a picture be repeated? Both viewpoints have many supporters. The probability is that repetition is an economy. We are after new customers always. It is not probable that they remember a picture we have used before. If they do, repetition does not detract.

Do color pictures pay better than black and white? Not generally, according to the evidence we have gathered to date. Yet there are exceptions. Certain food dishes look far better in colors. Tests on lines like oranges, desserts, etc. show that color pays. Color comes close to placing the products on actual exhibition.

But color used to amuse or to gain attention is like anything else that we use for that purpose. It may attract many times as many people, yet not secure a hearing from as many whom we want.

The general rule applies. Do nothing to merely interest, amuse, or attract. That is not your province. Do only that which wins the people you are after in the cheapest possible way.

But these are minor questions. They are mere economies, not largely affecting the results of a campaign.

Some things you do may cut all your results in two. Other things can be done which multiply those results. Minor costs are insignificant when compared with basic principles. One man may do

CHAPTER TEN

Things
too costly

M any things are possible in advertising which
are too costly to attempt. That is another
reason why every project and method should be
weighed and determined by a known scale of cost
and result.

Changing people's habits is very expensive. A
project which involves that must be seriously considered. To sell shaving soap to the peasants of
Russia one would first need to change their beard-
wearing habits. The cost would be excessive. Yet
countless advertisers try to do things almost as impossible. Just because questions are not ably considered, and results are untraced and unknown.

For instance, the advertiser of a dentifrice may
spend much space and money to educate people
to brush their teeth. Tests which we know of have

indicated that the cost of such converts may run from $20 to $25 each. Not only because of the difficulty, but because much of the advertising goes to people already converted.

Such a cost, of course, is unthinkable. One might not in a lifetime get it back in sales. The maker who learned these facts by tests makes no attempt to educate people to the tooth brush habit. What cannot be done on a large scale profitably cannot be done on a small scale. So not one line in any ad is devoted to this object. This maker, who is constantly guided in everything by keying every ad, has made a remarkable success.

Another dentifrice maker spends much money to make converts to the tooth brush. The object is commendable, but altruistic. The new business he creates is shared by his rivals. He is wondering why his sales increase is in no way commensurate with his expenditure.

An advertiser at one time spent much money to educate people to the use of oatmeal. The results were too small to discover. All people know of oatmeal. As a food for children it has age-old fame. Doctors have advised it for many generations. People who don't serve oatmeal are therefore difficult to start. Perhaps their objections are insurmountable. Anyway, the cost proved to be beyond all possible return.

There are many advertisers who know facts like these and concede them. They would not think of devoting a whole campaign to any such impossible object. Yet they devote a share of their space to that object. That is only the same folly on a smaller scale. It is not good business.

No one orange grower or raisin grower could attempt to increase the consumption of those fruits. The cost might be a thousand times his share of the returns. But thousands of growers combined have done it on those and many other lines. There lies one of the great possibilities of advertising development. The general consumption of scores of foods can be profitably increased. But it must be done through wide co-operation.

No advertiser could afford to educate people on vitamins or germicides. Such things are done by authorities, through countless columns of un-paid-for space. But great successes have been made by going to people already educated and satisfying their created wants.

It is a very shrewd thing to watch the development of a popular trend, the creation of new desires. Then at the right time offer to satisfy those desires. That was done on yeasts, for instance, and on numerous antiseptics. It can every year be done on new things which some popular fashion or widespread influence is bringing into vogue. But it is a very different thing to create that fashion, taste or influence for all in your field to share.

There are some things we know of which might possibly be sold to half the homes in the country.

A Dakin-fluid germicide, for instance. But the consumption would be very small. A small bottle might last for years. Customers might cost $1.50 each. And the revenue per customer might not in ten years repay the cost of getting.

Mail order sales on single articles, however popular, rarely cost less than $2.50 each. It is reasonable to suppose that sales made through dealers on like articles will cost approximately as much. Those facts must be considered on any one-sale article. Possibly one user will win others. But traced returns as in mail order advertising would prohibit much advertising which is now being done.

Costly mistakes are made by blindly following some ill-conceived idea. An article, for instance, may have many uses, one of which is to prevent disease. Prevention is not a popular subject, however much it should be. People will do much to cure a trouble, but people in general will do little to prevent it. This has been proved by many disappointments.

One may spend much money in arguing prevention when the same money spent on another claim would bring many times the sales. A heading which asserts one claim may bring ten times the results of a heading which asserts another. An advertiser may go far astray unless he finds this out.

A tooth paste may tend to prevent decay. It may also beautify the teeth. Tests will probably show that the latter appeal is many times as strong as the former. The most successful tooth paste advertiser never features tooth troubles in his headlines. Tests have proved them unappealing. Other advertisers in this line center on those troubles. That is often because results are not known and compared.

A soap may tend to cure eczema. It may at the same time improve the complexion. The eczema claim may appeal to one in a hundred while the beauty claims would appeal to nearly all. To even mention the eczema claims might destroy the beauty claim.

A man has a relief for asthma. It has done so much for him that he considers it a great advertising possibility. We have no statistics on this subject. We do not know the percentage of people who suffer from asthma. A canvass might show it to be one in a hundred. If so, he would need to cover a hundred useless readers to reach the one he wants. His cost of results might be twenty times as high as on another article which appeals to one in five. That excessive cost would probably mean disaster. For reasons like these every new advertiser should seek for wise advice. No one with the interests of advertising at heart will advise any dubious venture.

Some claims not popular enough to feature in the main are still popular enough to consider. They influence a certain number of people—say one-fourth of your possible customers. Such a claim may be featured to advantage in a certain percentage of headlines. It should probably be included in every advertisement. But those are not things to guess at. They should be decided by actual knowledge, usually by traced returns.

This chapter, like every chapter, points out a very important reason for knowing your results. Scientific advertising is impossible without that. So is safe advertising. So is maximum profit.

Groping in the dark in this field has probably cost enough money to pay the national debt. That is what has filled the advertising graveyards. That is what has discouraged thousands who could profit in this field. And the dawn of knowledge is what is bringing a new day in the advertising world.

CHAPTER ELEVEN

Information

An ad-writer, to have a chance at success, must gain full information on his subject. The library of an advertising agency should have books on every line that calls for research. A painstaking advertising man will often read for weeks on some problem which comes up.

Perhaps in many volumes he will find few facts to use. But some one fact may be the keynote of success.

This writer has just completed an enormous amount of reading, medical and otherwise, on coffee. This to advertise a coffee without caffeine. One scientific article out of a thousand perused gave the keynote for that campaign. It was the fact that caffeine stimulation comes two hours after drinking. So the immediate bracing effects which people seek from coffee do not come from the caffeine. Removing caffeine does not remove the kick. It does not modify coffee's delights, for caffeine is tasteless and odorless.

Caffeineless coffee has been advertised for years. People regarded it like near-beer. Only through weeks of reading did we find the way to put it in another light.

To advertise a tooth paste this writer has also read many volumes of scientific matter dry as dust. But in the middle of one volume he found the idea which has helped make millions for that tooth paste maker. And has made this campaign one of the sensations of advertising.

Genius is the art of taking pains. The advertising man who spares the midnight oil will never get very far.

Before advertising a food product, 130 men were employed for weeks to interview all classes of consumers.

On another line, letters were sent to 12,000 physicians. Questionnaires are often mailed to tens of thousands of men and women to get the viewpoint of consumers.

A $25,000-a-year man, before advertising outfits for acetylene gas, spent weeks in going from farm to farm. Another man did that on a tractor.

Before advertising a shaving cream, one thousand men were asked to state what they most desired in shaving soap.

Called on to advertise pork and beans, a canvass was made of some thousands of homes. Theretofore all pork and bean advertising had been based on "Buy my brand." That canvass showed that only 4 per cent of the people used any canned pork and beans. Ninety-six per cent baked their beans at home.

The problem was not to sell a particular brand. Any such attempt appealed to only four per cent. The right appeal was to win the people away from home-baked beans. That advertising, which without that knowledge must have failed, proved a great success.

A canvass is made, not only of homes, but of dealers. Competition is measured up.

Every advertiser of a similar product is written for his literature and claims. Thus we start with exact information on all that our rivals are doing.

Clipping bureaus are patronized, so that everything printed on our subject comes to the man who writes ads.

Every comment which comes from consumers or dealers goes to this man's desk.

It is often necessary in a line to learn the total expenditure. We must learn what a user spends a year, else we shall not know if users are worth the cost of getting.

We must learn the total consumption, else we may overspend.

We must learn the percentage of readers to whom our product appeals. We must often gather this data on classes. The percentage may differ on farms and in cities. The cost of advertising largely depends on the percentage of waste circulation.

Thus an advertising campaign is usually preceded by a very large volume of data. Even an experimental campaign, for effective experiments cost a great deal of work and time.

Often chemists are employed to prove or disprove doubtful claims. An advertiser, in all good faith, makes an impressive assertion. If it is true, it will form a big factor in advertising. If untrue, it may prove a boomerang. And it may bar our ads from good mediums. It is remarkable how often a maker proves wrong on assertions he has made for years.

Impressive claims are made far more impressive by making them exact. So many experiments are often made to get the actual figures. For instance, a certain drink is known to have a large food value. That simple assertion is not very convincing. So we send the drink to a laboratory and find that its food value is 425 calories per pint. One pint is equal to six eggs in calories of nutriment. That claim makes a great impression.

In every line involving scientific details a censor is appointed. The ad-writer, however well informed, may draw wrong inferences from facts. So an authority passes on every advertisement.

The uninformed would be staggered to know the amount of work involved in a single ad. Weeks of work sometimes. The ad seems so simple, and it must be simple to appeal to simple people. But back of that ad may lie reams of data, volumes of information, months of research.

So this is no lazy man's field.

CHAPTER TWELVE

Strategy

Advertising is much like war, minus the venom. Or much, if you prefer, like a game of chess. We are usually out to capture others' citadels or garner others' trade.

We must have skill and knowledge. We must have training and experience, also right equipment. We must have proper ammunition, and enough. We dare not underestimate opponents. Our intelligence department is a vital factor, as told in the previous chapter. We need alliances with dealers, as another chapter tells. We also need strategy of the ablest sort, to multiply the value of our forces.

Sometimes in new campaigns comes the question of a name. That may be most important. Often the right name is an advertisement in itself. It may tell a fairly complete story, like Shredded Wheat,

Cream of Wheat, Puffed Rice, Spearmint Gum, Palmolive Soap, etc.

That may be a great advantage. The name is usually conspicuously displayed. Many a name has proved to be the greatest factor in an article's success. Other names prove a distinct disadvantage—Toasted Corn Flakes, for instance. Too many others may share a demand with the man who builds it up.

Many coined names without meaning have succeeded. Kodak, Karo, Mazda, etc., are examples. They are exclusive. The advertiser who gives them meaning never needs to share his advantage. But a significant name which helps to impress a dominant claim is certainly a great advantage. Names which tell stories have been worth millions of dollars. So a great deal of research often precedes the selection of a name.

Sometimes a price must be decided. A high price creates resistance. It tends to limit one's field. The cost of getting an added profit may be more than the profit.

It is a well-known fact that the greatest profits are made on great volume at small profit. Campbell's Soups, Palmolive Soap, Karo Syrup and Ford cars are conspicuous examples. A price which appeals only to—say 10 per cent—multiplies the cost of selling.

But on other lines high price is unimportant. High profit is essential. The line may have small sale per customer. One hardly cares what he pays for a corn remedy because he uses little. The maker must have a large margin because of small consumption.

On other lines a higher price may be even an inducement. Such lines are judged largely by price. A product which costs more than the ordinary is considered above the ordinary. So the price question is always a very big factor in strategy.

Competition must be considered. What are the forces against you? What have they in price or quality or claims to weigh against your appeal? What have you to win trade against them? What have you to hold trade against them when you get it?

How strongly are your rivals entrenched? There are some fields which are almost inpregnable. They are usually lines which created a new habit or custom and which typify that custom with consumers. They so dominate a field that one can hardly hope to invade it. They have the volume, the profit to make a tremendous fight.

Such fields are being constantly invaded. But it is done through some convincing advantage, or through very superior salesmanship-in-print.

Other lines are only less difficult. A new shaving soap, as an example. About every possible customer is using some rival soap. Most of them are satisfied with it. Many are wedded to it. The appeal must be strong enough to win those people from long-established favor.

Such things are not accomplished by haphazard efforts. Not by considering people in the mass and making blind stabs for their favors. We must consider individuals, typical people who are using rival brands. A man on a Pullman, for instance, using his favorite soap. What could you say to him in person to get him to change to yours? We cannot go after thousands of men until we learn how to win one.

The maker may say that he has no distinctions. He is making a good product, but much like others. He deserves a share of the trade, but he has nothing exclusive to offer. However, there is nearly always something impressive which others have not told. We must discover it. We must have a seeming advantage. People don't quit habits without reason.

There is the problem of substitution and how to head it off. That often steals much of one's trade. This must be considered in one's original plan. One must have the foresight to see all eventualities, and the wisdom to establish his defenses in advance.

Many pioneers in a line establish large demands. Then, through some fault in their foundations, lose a large share of the harvest. Theirs is a mere brand, for instance, where it might have stood for an exclusive product.

Vaseline is an example. That product established a new demand, then almost monopolized that demand through wisdom at the start. To have called it some brand of petroleum jelly might have made a difference of millions in results.

Jell-O, Postum, Victrola, Kodak, etc., established coined names which came to typify a product. Some such names have been admitted to the dictionary. They have become common names, though coined and exclusive.

Royal Baking Powder and Toasted Corn Flakes, on the other hand, when they pioneered their fields, left the way open to perpetual substitution. So did Horlick's Malted Milk.

The attitude of dealers must be considered. There is a growing inclination to limit lines, to avoid duplicate lines, to lessen inventories. If this applies to your line, how will dealers receive it? If there is opposition, how can we circumvent it?

The problems of distribution are important and enormous. To advertise something which few dealers supply is a waste of ammunition. Those problems will be considered in a separate chapter.

These are samples of the problems which advertising men must solve. These are some of the reasons why vast experience is necessary. One oversight may cost the client millions in the end. One wrong piece of strategy may prohibit success. Things done in one way may be twice as easy, half as costly, as when done another way.

Advertising without this preparation is like a waterfall going to waste. The power may be there, but it is not made effective. We must center the force and direct it in a practical direction.

Advertising often looks very simple. Thousands of men claim ability to do it. And there still is a wide impression that many men can. As a result, much advertising goes by favor. But the men who know realize that the problems are as many and as important as the problems in building a skyscraper. And many of them lie in the foundations.

CHAPTER THIRTEEN

Use of samples

The product itself should be its own best salesman. Not the product alone, but the product
plus a mental impression, and atmosphere, which
you place around it. That being so, samples are of
prime importance. However expensive, they usually form the cheapest selling method. A salesman
might as well go out without his sample case as
an advertiser.

Sampling does not apply to little things alone,
like foods or proprietaries. It can be applied in some
way to almost anything. We have sampled clothing.
We are now sampling phonograph records.

Samples serve numerous valuable purposes.
They enable one to use the word "Free" in ads.
That often multiplies the readers. Most people
want to learn about any offered gift. Tests often

show that samples pay for themselves—perhaps several times over—in multiplying the readers of your ads without additional cost of space.

A sample gets action. The reader of your ad may not be convinced to the point of buying. But he is ready to learn more about the product that you offer. So he cuts out a coupon, lays it aside, and later mails it or presents it. Without that coupon he would soon forget.

Then you have the name and address of an interested prospect. You can start him using your product. You can give him fuller information. You can follow him up.

That reader might not again read one of your ads in six months. Your impression would be lost. But when he writes you, you have a chance to complete with that prospect all that can be done. In that saving of waste the sample pays for itself.

Sometimes a small sample is not a fair test. Then we may send an order on the dealer for a full-size package. Or we may make the coupon good for a package at the store. Thus we get a longer test.

You say that is expensive. So is it expensive to gain a prospect's interest. It may cost you 50 cents to get the person to the point of writing for a sample. Don't stop at 15 cents additional to make that interest valuable.

Another way in which samples pay is by keying your advertisements. They register the interest you create. Thus you can compare one with another ad, headline, plan and method.

That means in any line an enormous saving. The wisest, most experienced man cannot tell what will most appeal in any line of copy. Without a key to guide you, your returns are very apt to cost you twice what they need cost. And we know that some ads on the same product will cost ten times what others cost. A sample may pay for itself several times over by giving you an accurate check.

Again samples enable you to refer customers where they can be supplied. This is important before you attain general distribution.

Many advertisers lose much by being pennywise. They are afraid of imposition, or they try to save pennies. That is why they ask ten cents for a sample, or a stamp or two. Getting that dime may cost them from 40 cents to $1. That is, it may add that to the cost of the replies. But it is remarkable how many will pay that addition rather than offer a sample free.

Putting a price on a sample greatly retards replies. Then it prohibits you from using the word "Free" in your ads. And that word "Free," as we have stated, will generally more than pay for your samples.

For the same reason some advertisers say, "You buy one package, we will buy the other." Or they make a coupon good for part of the purchase price. Any keyed returns will clearly prove that such offers do not pay. Before a prospect is converted, it is approximately as hard to get half price for your article as to get the full price for it.

Bear in mind that you are the seller. You are the one courting interest. Then don't make it difficult to exhibit that interest. Don't ask your prospects to pay for your selling efforts. Three in four will refuse to pay—perhaps nine in ten.

Cost of requests for samples differ in every line. It depends on your breadth of appeal. Some things appeal to everybody, some to a small percentage. One issue of the papers in Greater New York brought 1,460,000 requests for a can of evaporated milk. On a chocolated drink, one-fifth the coupons published are presented. Another line not widely used may bring a fraction of that number.

But the cost of inquiries is usually enough to be important. Then don't neglect them. Don't stint your efforts with those you have half sold. An inquiry means that a prospect has read your story and is interested. He or she would like to try your product and learn more about it. Do what you would do if that prospect stood before you.

Cost of inquiries depends largely on how they come. Asking people to mail the coupon brings minimum returns. Often four times as many will present that coupon for a sample at the store.

On a line before the writer now, sample inquiries obtained by mail average 70 cents each. The same ads bring inquiries at from 18 cents to

22 cents each when the coupons are presented at a local store.

Most people write few letters. Writing is an effort. Perhaps they have no stamps in the house. Most people will pay carfare to get a sample rather than two cents postage. Therefore, it is always best, where possible, to have samples delivered locally.

On one line three methods were offered. The woman could write for a sample, or telephone, or call at a store. Seventy per cent of the inquiries came by telephone. The use of the telephone is more common and convenient than the use of stamps.

Sometimes it is not possible to supply all dealers with samples. Then we refer people to some central stores. These stores are glad to have many people come there. And other dealers do not generally object so long as they share in the sales.

It is important to have these dealers send you the coupons promptly. Then you can follow up the inquiries while their interest is fresh.

It is said that sample users repeat. They do to some extent. But repeaters form a small percentage. Figure it in your cost.

Say to the woman, "Only one sample to a home" and few women will try to get more of them. And the few who cheat you are not generally people who would buy. So you are not losing purchasers, but the samples only.

On numerous lines we have for long offered full-size packages free. The packages were priced at from 10 cents to 50 cents each. In certain territories for a time we have checked up on repeaters. And we found the loss much less than the cost of checking.

In some lines samples would be wasted on children, and they are most apt to get them. Then say in your coupon "adults only." Children will not present such coupons, and they will rarely mail them.

But one must be careful about publishing coupons good for a full-size package at any store. Some people, and even dealers, may buy up many papers. We do not announce the date of such offers. And we insert them in Sunday papers, not so easily bought up.

But we do not advocate samples given out promiscuously. Samples distributed to homes, like waifs on the doorsteps, probably never pay. Many of them never reach the housewife. When they do, there is no predilection for them. The product is cheapened. It is not introduced in a favorable way.

So with demonstrations in stores. There is always a way to get the same results at a fraction of the cost.

Many advertisers do not understand this. They supply thousands of samples to dealers to be handed out as they will. Could a trace be placed on the cost of returns, the advertiser would be stunned.

Give samples to interested people only. Give them only to people who exhibit that interest by some effort. Give them only to people to whom you have told your story. First create an atmosphere of respect, a desire, an expectation. When people are in that mood, your sample will usually confirm the qualities you claim.

Here again comes the advantage of figuring cost per customer. That is the only way to gauge advertising. Samples sometimes seem to double advertising cost. They often cost more than the advertising. Yet, rightly used, they almost invariably form the cheapest way to get customers. And that is what you want.

The arguments against samples are usually biased. They may come from advertising agents who like to see all the advertising money spent in print. Answer such arguments by tests. Try some towns with them, some without them. Where samples are effectively employed, we rarely find a line where they do not lessen the cost per customer.

CHAPTER FOURTEEN

Getting
distribution

Most advertisers are confronted with the problem of getting distribution. National advertising is unthinkable without that. A venture cannot be profitable if nine in ten of the converts fail to find the goods.

To force dealers to stock by bringing repeated demands may be enormously expensive. To cover the country with a selling force is usually impossible. To get dealers to stock an unknown line on promise of advertising is not easy. They have seen too many efforts fail, too many promises rescinded.

We cannot discuss all plans for getting distribution. There are scores of ways employed, according to the enterprise. Some start by soliciting direct sales—mail orders—until the volume of demand forces dealers to supply.

Some get into touch with prospects by a sample or other offer, then refer them to certain dealers who are stocked.

Some well-known makers can get a large percentage of dealers to stock in advance under guarantee of sale. Some consign goods to jobbers so dealers can easily order. Some name certain dealers in their ads until dealers in general stock.

The problems in this line are numberless. The successful methods are many. But most of them apply to lines too few to be worthy of discussion in a book like this.

We shall deal here with articles of wide appeal and repeated sales, like foods or proprietary articles.

We usually start with local advertising, even though magazine advertising is best adapted to the article. We get our distribution town by town, then change to national advertising.

Sometimes we name the dealers who are stocked. As others stock, we add their names. When a local campaign is proposed, naming certain dealers, the average dealer wants to be included. It is often possible to get most of them by offering to name them in the first few ads.

Whether you advertise few or many dealers, the others will stock in very short order if the advertising is successful. Then the trade is referred to all dealers.

The sample plans dealt with in the previous chapter aid quick distribution. They often pay for themselves in this way alone.

If the samples are distributed locally, the coupon names the stores. The prospects who go there to get samples know that those stores are supplied, if a nearer dealer is not. Thus little trade is lost.

When sample inquiries come to the advertiser, inquirers are referred to certain dealers at the start. Enough demand is centered there to force those dealers to supply it.

Sometimes most stores are supplied with samples, but on the requirement of a certain purchase. You supply a dozen samples with a dozen packages, for instance. Then inquirers for samples are referred to all stores. This quickly forces general distribution. Dealers don't like to have their customers go to competitors even for a sample.

Where a coupon is used, good at any store for a full-size package, the problem of distribution becomes simple. Mail to dealers proofs of the ad which will contain the coupon. Point out to each that many of his customers are bound to present that coupon. Each coupon means a cash sale at full profit. No average dealer will let those coupon customers go elsewhere.

Such a free-package offer often pays for itself in this way. It forms the cheapest way of getting general distribution.

Some of the most successful advertisers have done this in a national way. They have inserted coupon ads in magazines, each coupon good at any store for a full-size package. A proof of the ad is sent to dealers in advance, with a list of the magazines to be used, and their circulation.

In this way, in one week sometimes, makers attain a reasonable national distribution. And the coupon ad, when it appears, completes it. Here again the free packages cost less than other ways of forcing distribution. And they start thousands of users besides. Palmolive Soap and Puffed Grains are among the products which attained their distribution in that way.

Half the circulation of a newspaper may go to outside towns. That half may be wasted if you offer a sample at local stores. Say in your coupon that outside people should write you for a sample. When they write, do not mail the sample. Send the samples to a local store, and refer inquirers to that store. Mailing a sample may make a convert who cannot be supplied. But the store which supplies the sample will usually supply demand.

In these ways, many advertisers get national distribution without employing a single salesman. They get it immediately. And they get it at far lower cost than by any other method.

There are advertisers who, in starting, send every dealer a few packages as a gift. That is better, perhaps, than losing customers created. But it is very expensive. Those free packages must be sold by advertising. Figure their cost at your selling price, and you will see that you are paying a high cost per dealer. A salesman might sell these small stocks at a lower cost. And other methods may be vastly cheaper.

Sending stocks on consignment to retailers is not widely favored. Many dealers resent it. Collections are difficult. And unbusinesslike methods do not win dealer respect.

The plans advocated here are the best plans yet discovered for the lines to which they apply. Other lines require different methods. The ramifications are too many to discuss in a book like this.

But don't start advertising without distribution. Don't get distribution by methods too expensive. Or by slow, old-fashioned methods. The loss of time may cost you enormously in sales. And it may enable energetic rivals to get ahead of you.

Go to men who know by countless experiences the best plan to apply to your line.

CHAPTER FIFTEEN

Test
campaigns

Almost any question can be answered, cheaply, quickly and finally, by a test campaign. And that's the way to answer them—not by arguments around a table. Go to the court of last resort—the buyers of your product.

On every new project there comes up the question of selling that article profitably. You and your friends may like it, but the majority may not. Some rival product may be better liked or cheaper. It may be strongly entrenched. The users won away from it may cost too much to get.

People may buy and not repeat. The article may last too long. It may appeal to a small percentage, so most of your advertising goes to waste.

There are many surprises in advertising. A project you will laugh at may make a great success. A

294

project you are sure of may fall down. All because tastes differ so. None of us know enough people's desires to get an average viewpoint.

In the old days, advertisers ventured on their own opinions. The few guessed right, the many wrong. Those were the times of advertising disasters. Even those who succeeded came close to the verge before the tide was turned. They did not know their cost per customer or their sale per customer. The cost of selling might take long to come back. Often it never came back.

Now we let the thousands decide what the millions will do. We make a small venture, and watch cost and result. When we learn what a thousand customers cost, we know almost exactly what a million will cost. When we learn what they buy, we know what a million will buy.

We establish averages on a small scale, and those averages always hold. We know our cost, we know our sale, we know our profit or our loss. We know how soon our cost comes back. Before we spread out, we prove our undertaking absolutely safe. So there are today no advertising disasters piloted by men who know.

Perhaps we try out our project in four or five towns. We may use a sample offer or a free package to get users started quickly. We learn in this way the cost per customer started. Then we wait and see if users buy those samples. If they do, will they continue? How much will they buy? How long does it take for the profit to return our cost of selling?

A test like this may cost $3,000 to $5,000. It is not all lost, even when the product proves unpopular. Some sales are made. Nearly every test will in time bring back the entire cost.

Sometimes we find that the cost of the advertising comes back before the bills are due. That means that the product can be advertised without investment. Many a great advertiser has been built up without any cost whatever beyond immediate receipts. That is an ideal situation.

On another product it may take three months to bring back the cost with a profit. But one is sure of his profit in that time. When he spreads out he must finance accordingly.

Think what this means. A man has what he considers an advertising possibility. But national advertising looks so big and expensive that he dare not undertake it.

Now he presents it in a few average towns, at a very modest cost. With almost no risk whatever. From the few thousands he learns what the millions will do. Then he acts accordingly. If he then branches out he knows to a certainty just what his results will be.

He is playing on the safe side of a hundred to one shot. If the article is successful, it may make him millions. If he is mistaken about it, the loss is a trifle.

These are facts we desire to emphasize and spread. All our largest accounts are now built in this way, from very small beginnings. When business men realize that this can be done, hundreds of others will do it. For countless fortune-earners now lie dormant.

The largest advertiser in the world makes a business of starting such projects. One by one he finds out winners. Now he has twenty-six, and together they earn many millions yearly.

These test campaigns have other purposes. They answer countless questions which arise in business.

A large food advertiser felt that his product would be more popular in another form. He and all his advisers were certain about it. They were willing to act on this supposition without consulting the consumers, but wiser advice prevailed.

He inserted an ad in a few towns with a coupon, good at any store for a package of the new-style product. Then he wrote to the users about it. They were almost unanimous in their disapproval.

Later the same product was suggested in still another form. The previous verdict made the change look dubious. The advertiser hardly thought a test worth while. But he submitted the question to a few thousand women in a similar way and 91 per cent voted for it. Now he has a unique product which promises to largely increase his sales.

These tests cost about $1,000 each. The first one saved him a very costly mistake. The second will probably bring him large profits.

Then we use test campaigns to try out new methods on advertising already successful. Thus we constantly seek for better methods, without interrupting plans already proved out.

In five years for one food advertiser we tried out over fifty separate plans. Every little while we found an improvement, so the results of our advertising constantly grew. At the end of five years we found the best plan of all. It reduced our cost of selling by 75 per cent. That is, it was four times more effective than the best plan used before.

That is what mail order advertisers do—try out plan after plan to constantly reduce the cost. Why should any general advertiser be less business-like and careful?

Another service of the test campaign is this:

An advertiser is doing mediocre advertising. A skilled advertising agent feels that he can greatly increase results. The advertiser is doubtful. He is doing fairly well. He has alliances which he hesitates to break. So he is inclined to let well enough alone.

Now the question can be submitted to the verdict of a test. The new agent may take a few towns, without interfering with the general campaign. Then compare his results with the general results and prove his greater skill.

Plausible arguments are easy in this line. One man after another comes to an advertiser to claim superior knowledge or ability. It is hard to decide, and decisions may be wrong.

Now actual figures gained at a small cost can settle the question definitely. The advertiser makes no commitment. It is like saying to a salesman, "Go out for a week and prove." A large percentage of all the advertising done would change hands if this method were applied.

Again we come back to scientific advertising. Suppose a chemist would say in an arbitrary way that this compound was best, or that better. You would little respect his opinion. He makes tests— sometimes hundreds of tests—to actually know which is best. He will never state a supposition before he has proved it. How long before advertisers in general will apply that exactness to advertising?

CHAPTER SIXTEEN

Leaning
on dealers

We cannot depend much in most lines on the active help of jobbers or of dealers. They are busy. They have many lines to consider. The profit on advertised lines is not generally large. And an advertised article is apt to be sold at cut prices.

The average dealer does what you would do. He exerts himself on brands of his own, if at all. Not on another man's brand.

The dealer will often try to make you think otherwise. He will ask some aid or concession on the ground of extra effort. Advertisers often give extra discounts. Or they make loading offers—perhaps one case free in ten—in the belief that loaded dealers will make extra efforts.

This may be so on rare lines, but not generally. And efforts if made do not usually increase the total sales. They merely swing trade from one store to another.

On most lines, making a sale without making a convert does not count for much. Sales made by conviction—by advertising—are likely to bring permanent customers. People who buy through casual recommendations do not often stick. Next time someone else gives other advice.

Revenue which belongs to the advertiser is often given away without adequate return. These discounts and gifts could be far better spent in securing new consumers.

Free goods must be sold, and by your own efforts usually. One extra case with ten means that advertising must sell ten per cent more to bring you the same return. The dealer would probably buy just as much if you let him buy as convenient.

Much money is often frittered away on other forms of dealer help. Perhaps on window or store displays. A window display, acting as a reminder, may bring to one dealer a lion's share of the trade. Yet it may not increase your total sales at all.

Those are facts to find out. Try one town in one way, one in another. Compare total sales in those towns. In many lines such tests will show that costly displays are worthless. A growing number of experienced advertisers spend no money on displays.

This is all in line of general publicity, so popular long ago. Casting bread upon the waters and hoping for its return. Most advertising was of that sort twenty years ago.

Now we put things to the test. We compare cost and result on every form of expenditure. It is easily done. Very many costly wastes are eliminated by this modern process.

Scientific advertising has altered many old plans and conceptions. It has proved many long-established methods to be folly. And why should we not apply to these things the same criterion we apply to other forms of selling? Or to manufacturing costs?

Your object in all advertising is to buy new customers at a price which pays a profit. You have no interest in centering trade at any particular store. Learn what your consumers cost and what they buy. If they cost you one dollar each, figure that every wasted dollar costs you a possible customer.

Your business will be built in that way, not by dealer help. You must do your own selling, make your own success. Be content if dealers fill the orders that you bring. Eliminate your wastes. Spend all your ammunition where it counts for most.

CHAPTER SEVENTEEN

Individuality

A person who desires to make an impression must stand out in some way from the masses. And in a pleasing way. Being eccentric, being abnormal is not a distinction to covet. But doing admirable things in a different way gives one a great advantage.

So with salesmen, in person or in print. There is uniqueness which belittles and arouses resentment. There is refreshing uniqueness which enhances, which we welcome and remember. Fortunate is the salesman who has it.

We try to give each advertiser a becoming style. We make him distinctive, perhaps not in appearance, but in manner and in tone. He is given an individuality best suited to the people he addresses.

One man appears rugged and honest in a line where rugged honesty counts. One may be a good fellow where choice is a matter of favor. In other lines the man stands out by impressing himself as an authority.

We have already cited a case where a woman made a great success in selling clothing to girls, solely through a created personality which won.

That's why we have signed ads sometimes—to give them a personal authority. A man is talking—a man who takes pride in his accomplishments—not a "soulless corporation." Whenever possible we introduce a personality into our ads. By making a man famous we make his product famous. When we claim an improvement, naming the man who made it adds effect.

Then we take care not to change an individuality which has proved appealing. Before a man writes a new ad on that line, he gets into the spirit adopted by the advertiser. He plays a part as an actor plays it.

In successful advertising great pains are taken to never change our tone. That which won so many is probably the best way to win others. Then people come to know us. We build on that acquaintance rather than introduce a stranger in strange guise. People do not know us by name alone, but by looks and mannerisms. Appearing different every time we meet never builds up confidence.

Then we don't want people to think that salesmanship is made to order. That our appeals are created, studied, artificial. They must seem to come from the heart, and the same heart always, save where a wrong tack forces a complete change.

There are winning personalities in ads as well as people. To some we are glad to listen, others bore us. Some are refreshing, some commonplace. Some inspire confidence, some caution.

To create the right individuality is a supreme accomplishment. Then an advertiser's growing rep-- utation on that line brings him ever-increasing prestige. Never weary of that part. Remember that a change in our characteristics would compel our best friends to get acquainted all over.

CHAPTER EIGHTEEN

Negative advertising

To attack a rival is never good advertising. Don't point out others' faults. It is not permitted in the best mediums. It is never good policy. The selfish purpose is apparent. It looks unfair, not sporty. If you abhor knockers, always appear a good fellow.

Show the bright side, the happy and attractive side, not the dark and uninviting side of things. Show beauty, not homeliness; health, not sickness. Don't show the wrinkles you propose to remove, but the face as it will appear. Your customers know all about the wrinkles.

In advertising a dentifrice, show pretty teeth, not bad teeth. Talk of coming good conditions, not conditions which exist. In advertising clothes, picture well-dressed people, not the shabby. Picture successful men, not failures, when you advertise a business course. Picture what others wish to be, not what they may be now.

We are attracted by sunshine, beauty, happiness, health, success. Then point the way to them, not the way out of the opposite.

Picture envied people, not the envious.

Tell people what to do, not what to avoid.

Make your every ad breathe good cheer. We always dodge a Lugubrious Blue.

Assume that people will do what you ask. Say, "Send now for this sample." Don't say, "Why do you neglect this offer?" That suggests that people are neglecting. Invite them to follow the crowd.

Compare the results of two ads, one negative, one positive. One presenting the dark side, one the bright side. One warning, the other inviting. You will be surprised. You will find that the positive ad outpulls the other four to one, if you have our experience.

The "Before and after taking" ads are follies of the past. They never had a place save with the afflicted. Never let their memory lead you to picture the gloomy side of things.

CHAPTER NINETEEN

Letter
writing

This is another phase of advertising which all of us have to consider. It enters, or should enter, into nearly all campaigns. Every business man receives a large number of circular letters. Most of them go direct to the waste basket. But he acts on others, and others are filed for reference.

Analyze those letters. The ones you act on or the ones you keep have a headline which attracted your interest. At a glance they offer something that you want, something you may wish to know.

Remember that point in all advertising.

A certain buyer spends $50,000,000 per year. Every letter, every circular which comes to his desk gets its deserved attention. He wants information on the lines he buys.

But we have often watched him. In one minute a score of letters may drop into the waste basket.

Then one is laid aside. That is something to consider at once. Another is filed under the heading "Varnish." And later when he buys varnish that letter will turn up.

That buyer won several prizes by articles on good buying. His articles were based on information. Yet the great masses of matter which came to him never got more than a glance.

The same principles apply to all advertising. Letter writers overlook them just as advertisers do. They fail to get the right attention. They fail to tell what buyers wish to know.

One magazine sends out millions of letters annually. Some to get subscriptions, some to sell books. Before the publisher sends out five million letters he puts a few thousands to test. He may try twenty-five letters, each with a thousand prospects. He learns what results will cost. Perhaps the plan is abandoned because it appears unprofitable. If not, the letter which pays best is the letter that he uses.

Just as men are doing now in all scientific advertising.

Mail order advertisers do likewise. They test their letters as they test their ads. A general letter is never used until it proves itself best among many by actual returns.

Letter writing has much to do with advertising. Letters to inquirers, follow-up letters. Wherever possible they should be tested. Where that is not possible, they should be based on knowledge gained by tests.

We find the same difference in letters as in ads. Some get action, some do not. Some complete a sale, some forfeit the impression gained. These letters, going usually to half-made converts, are tremendously important.

Experience generally shows that a two-cent letter gets no more attention than a one-cent letter. Fine stationery no more than poor stationery. The whole appeal lies in the matter.

It has been found that fine stationery and pamphlets lessen the effect. They indicate an effort to sell on other lines than merit. That has the same effect in letters as in ads.

A letter which goes to an inquirer is like a salesman going to an interested prospect. You know what created that interest. Then follow it up along that line, not on some different argument. Complete the impression already created. Don't undertake another on a guess.

In a letter as in ads, the great point is to get immediate action. People are naturally dilatory. They postpone, and a postponed action is too often forgotten.

Do something if possible to get immediate action. Offer some inducement for it. Or tell what delay may cost. Note how many successful selling letters place a limit on an offer. It expires on a certain date. That is all done to get a prompt decision, to overcome the tendency to delay.

A mail order advertiser offered a catalog. The inquirer might send for three or four similar catalogs. He had that competition in making a sale.

So he wrote a letter when he sent his catalog, and enclosed a personal card. He said, "You are a new customer, and we want to make you welcome. So when you send your order please enclose this card. The writer wants to see that you get a gift with the order—something you can keep."

With an old customer he gave some other reason for the gift. The offer aroused curiosity. It gave preference to his catalog. Without some compelling reason for ordering elsewhere, the woman sent the order to him. The gift paid for itself several times over by bringing larger sales per catalog.

The ways for getting action are many. Rarely can one way be applied to two lines. But the principles are universal. Strike while the iron is hot. Get a decision then. Have it followed by prompt action when you can.

You can afford to pay for prompt action rather than lose by delay. One advertiser induced hundreds of thousands of women to buy six packages of his product and send him the trademarks, to secure a premium offer good only for one week.

A name
that helps

There is great advantage in a name that tells a story. The name is usually prominently displayed. To justify the space it occupies, it should aid the advertising. Some such names are almost complete advertisements in themselves. May Breath is such a name. Cream of Wheat is another. That name alone has been worth a fortune. Other examples are Dutch Cleanser, Cuticura, Dyanshine, Minute Tapioca, 3-in-One Oil, Holeproof, Alcorub, etc.

Such names may be protected, yet the name itself describes the product, so it makes a valuable display.

Other coined names are meaningless. Some examples are Kodak, Karo, Mazda, Sapolio, Vaseline, Kotex, Lux, Postum, etc. They can be protected, and long-continued advertising may give them a meaning. When this is accomplished they become very valuable. But the great majority of them never attain that status.

Such names do not aid the advertising. It is very doubtful if they justify display. The service of the product, not the name, is the important thing in advertising. A vast amount of space is wasted in displaying names and pictures which tell no selling story. The tendency of modern advertising is to eliminate this waste.

Other coined names signify ingredients which anyone may use. Examples are Syrup of Figs, Cocoanut Oil Shampoo, Tar Soap, Palmolive Soap, etc.

Such products may dominate a market if the price is reasonable, but they must to a degree meet competition. They invite substitution. They are naturally classified with other products which have like ingredients, so the price must remain in that class.

Toasted Corn Flakes and Malted Milk are examples of unfortunate names. In each of those cases one advertiser created a new demand. When the demand was created, others shared it because they could use the name. The originators depended only on a brand. It is interesting to speculate on how much more profitable a coined name might have been.

On a patented product it must be remembered that the right to a name expires with the patent.

Names like Castoria, Aspirin, Shredded Wheat Biscuit, etc., have become common property.

This is a very serious point to consider. It often makes a patent an undesirable protection.

Another serious fault in coined names is frivolity. In seeking uniqueness one gets something trivial. And that is a fatal handicap in a serious product. It almost prohibits respect.

When a product must be called by a common name, the best auxiliary name is a man's name. It is much better than a coined name, for it shows that some man is proud of his creation.

Thus the question of a name is of serious importance in laying the foundations of a new undertaking. Some names have become the chief factors in success. Some have lost for their originators four-fifths of the trade they developed.

CHAPTER TWENTY-ONE

Good
business

A rapid stream ran by the writer's boyhood home. The stream turned a wooden wheel and the wheel ran a mill. Under that primitive method, all but a fraction of the stream's potentiality went to waste.

Then someone applied scientific methods to that stream—put in a turbine and dynamos. Now, with no more water, no more power, it runs a large manufacturing plant.

We think of that stream when we see wasted advertising power. And we see it everywhere— hundreds of examples. Enormous potentialities— millions of circulation—used to turn a mill-wheel. While others use that same power with manifold effect.

We see countless ads running year after year which we know to be unprofitable. Men spending five dollars to do what one dollar might do. Men getting back 30 per cent of their cost when they might get 150 per cent. And the facts could be easily proved.

We see wasted space, frivolity, clever conceits, entertainment. Costly pages filled with palaver which, if employed by a salesman, would reflect on his sanity. But those ads are always unkeyed. The money is spent blindly, merely to satisfy some advertising whim.

Not new advertisers only. Many an old advertiser has little or no idea of his advertising results. The business is growing through many efforts combined, and advertising is given its share of the credit.

An advertiser of many years' standing, spending as high as $700,000 per year, told the writer he did not know whether his advertising was worth anything or not. Sometimes he thought that his business would be just as large without it.

The writer replied, "I do know. Your advertising is utterly unprofitable, and I could prove it to you in one week. End an ad with an offer to pay five dollars to anyone who writes you that he read the ad through. The scarcity of replies will amaze you."

Think what a confession—that millions of dollars are being spent without knowledge of results. Such a policy applied to all factors in a business would bring ruin in short order.

You see other ads which you may not like as well. They may seem crowded or verbose. They are not attractive to you, for you are seeking something to admire, something to entertain. But you will note that those ads are keyed. The advertiser knows that they pay. The probability is that out of scores of traced ads the type which you see has paid best.

Many other ads which are not keyed now were keyed at the beginning. They are based on known statistics. They won on a small scale before they ever ran on a large scale. Those advertisers are utilizing their enormous powers in full.

Advertising is prima facie evidence that the man who pays believes that advertising is good. It has brought great results to others, it must be good for him. So he takes it like some secret tonic which others have endorsed. If the business thrives, the tonic gets the credit. Otherwise, the failure is due to fate.

That seems almost unbelievable. Even a storekeeper who inserts a twenty-dollar ad knows whether it pays or not. Every line of a big store's ad is charged to the proper department. And every inch used must the next day justify its cost.

Yet most national advertising is done without justification. It is merely presumed to pay. A little test might show a way to multiply returns.

Such methods, still so prevalent, are not very far from their end. The advertising men who practice them see the writing on the wall. The time is fast coming when men who spend money are going to know what they get. Good business and efficiency will be applied to advertising. Men and methods will be measured by the known returns, and only competent men can survive.

Only one hour ago an old advertising man said to the writer, "The day for our type is done. Bunk has lost its power. Sophistry is being displaced by actuality. And I tremble at the trend."

So do hundreds tremble. Enormous advertising is being done along scientific lines. Its success is common knowledge. Advertisers along other lines will not much longer be content.

We who can meet the test welcome these changed conditions. Advertisers will multiply when they see that advertising can be safe and sure. Small expenditures made on a guess will grow to big ones on a certainty. Our line of business will be finer, cleaner, when the gamble is removed. And we shall be prouder of it when we are judged on merit.